Political Babble

The 1,000 Dumbest Things
Ever Said by Politicians

DAVID OLIVE

Illustrated by Barry Blitt

John Wiley & Sons, Inc.

New York ♦ Chichester ♦ Brisbane ♦ Toronto ♦ Singapore

To my friend from the Crescent Beach, who had "no slight or trivial influence / On that best portion of a good man's life."

In recognition of the importance of preserving what has been written, it is a policy of John Wiley & Sons, Inc., to have books of enduring value published in the United States printed on acid-free paper, and we exert our best efforts to that end.

Library of Congress Cataloging-in-Publication Data
Olive, David.
    Political babble : the 1,000 dumbest things ever said by politicians /
David Olive : illustrated by Barry Blitt.
        p.   cm.
    ISBN 0-471-57710-3
    1. Political science—Humor.   2. Political science—Quotations,
maxims, etc.   3. United States—Politics and government—1989—
Humor.   4. United States—Politics and government—1989—Quotations, maxims, etc.   5. United States—Politics and government—1981–
1989—Humor.   6. United States—Politics and government—1981–
1989—Quotations, maxims, etc.   I. Title.
PN6231.P6055   1992
081—dc20   92-6331

Printed in the United States of America
10 9 8 7 6 5 4 3 2 1

The first mistake in public business is the going into it.

BENJAMIN FRANKLIN

Contents

Preface

Politics and the fate of mankind are formed by men without ideals and without greatness. Those who have greatness within them do not go in for politics.

ALBERT CAMUS, Notebooks (1935–1942)

I think we're on the road to coming up with answers that I don't think any of us in total feel we have the answers to.

KIM ANDERSON, mayor of Naples, Florida (1991)

We know Will Rogers was right in saying that it's easy to be a humorist when you have the entire government working for you. Fumbling verbosity in public life is as old as, well, public life. If there had been taped press conferences and boom microphones to record the verbal inanities and mendacities of Cicero, Louis XIV, and George Washington, this book would likely be of encyclopedic heft. But what exactly is it that reduces political activity to a parade of absurdities? Is it true, as Camus felt, that only those who are least worthy of political leadership aspire to it? Or is it fairer to say—for those who still suspect goodwill in some of our representatives—that "the hardest thing about any political campaign," as Adlai Stevenson said, "is how to win without proving that you are unworthy of winning"?

There are several reasons why people whom we would otherwise feel comfortable entrusting with the care of our children are transformed by the political process into stumbling dolts or fugitives from the truth whom we would not invite into our homes without first counting the silver.

For starters, candor, a quality much becoming of priests and psychiatrists, is not a valuable tool in the advancement of a political career. The People say they want truth, but the office-seeker knows voters are prepared only to accept a version of the truth that makes them feel good. Thus prevarication is, and always has been, a necessary first step on the road to success in public life.

We must consider also the pressure of the campaign trail, which—despite the obvious effects of sleep deprivation—demands memorable, pithy slogans. These predate the era of television: Louis XIV's assertion that "L'etat, c'est moi" was not made for the benefit of the cameras. But, of course, monarchs aren't tested at the polls.

Finally, there are the pressures of the office itself, which the hapless office-seeker often realizes he or she isn't equal to. Some political aspirants sense this earlier in their careers than others. Seven years before he took up residence in the White House, Ronald Reagan confessed, "The thought of being President frightens me and I do not think I want the job." No sooner had the seriously incompetent Warren Harding been installed in the Oval Office than he allowed that, "I am a man of limited talents from a small town. I don't seem to grasp that I am President."

The legacy of illustrious predecessors often tends to intimidate newcomers. Quite correctly, Gerald Ford adduced that he was not sufficiently gifted to handle the duties of an office that has occasionally been occupied by men of towering capabilities. "If Lincoln were alive today," Ford said soon after becoming president, "he'd roll over in his grave." Just so. With a keen sense of his own limitation, George Bush's man-child

Vice President Dan Quayle has allowed that, "I would rather have been a professional golfer, but my family pushed me into politics."

When the historian Barbara Tuchman, author of *The March of Folly*, wrote in 1980 that "government remains the paramount field of unwisdom," she reminded us that political life does not always attract the best and brightest candidates. Too often it has been a refuge for ambitious orators and favor-grantors whose principal recommendation for high office is that they lack the requisite qualifications for careers in which they would pose less of a hazard to society, such as law, performance art, or small-appliance repair.

Given the lack of training required of public officials, we should not be surprised when they exhibit a manifest inexpertise in matters of economic or historical knowledge—areas that are commonly the subject of more informed conversation in barber shops than in the halls of political power. "Fascism was really the basis of the New Deal," Ronald Reagan wanted us to understand in 1976—and this should have been the tip-off for what was to come, including the assessment by President Reagan's fan Margaret Thatcher in 1983: "It's a pity about Ronnie—he just doesn't understand economics at all."

Geography and foreign affairs also reveal a thousand points of political unenlightenment and seemed to have given the Reagan White House even greater difficulties. In 1982, describing how his recent trip to Latin America had changed his outlook on the region, the President explained, "You'd be surprised. They're all individual countries."

Of course, ignorance of foreign affairs knows no national boundaries. In 1991, former French prime minister Edith Cresson said of the Japanese, who must be a nation of insomniacs: "They sit up all night thinking of ways to screw the Americans and Europeans." In 1990, Italian porn star and member of Parliament Ilona (Cicciolina) Staller, in what may have been a diplomatic tip to George Bush, said: "I am available to make love with Saddam Hussein to achieve peace in the Middle East."

One thing that might help restore faith in our political officials is their capacity to grow in office. During a 1992 reelection campaign visit to a Head Start center in Maryland, George Bush demonstrated this marvelous ability to absorb new ideas. "And let me say in conclusion, thanks for the kids. I learned an awful lot about bathtub toys—about how to work the telephone. One guy knows—several of them know their own phone numbers—preparation to go to the dentist. A lot of things I'd forgotten." After becoming vice president, Dan Quayle also seemed to have grasped some larger truths. "What a waste it is to lose one's mind," he reflected in an address to the United Negro College Fund, "or not to have a mind. How true that is."

One of the trials of leadership is that the leader's faults cannot be hidden, and comments and beliefs we find tolerable and even amusing as imparted by friends in a pub are magnified and ridiculed, sometimes around the world, when they issue from the holder of a high office. And yet we must recognize that the assessment made by the editor of the Soviet weekly *Ogonyok* in 1988—"Reagan is a simple man, a normal man. We see this normal man and we want to have a normal man as the leader of our State"—explains the unlikely appeal of a great many leaders around the world. As Nebraska senator Roman Hruska said in 1970, defending President Nixon's nomination of Harrold Carswell to the Supreme Court, "Even if he were mediocre, there are a lot of mediocre judges and people and lawyers, and they are entitled to a little representation, aren't they?"

Perhaps the leadership principles reflected in this collection are what we're entitled to—indeed, what we deserve. "Democracy," H. L. Mencken said, "is the theory that the common people know what they want, and deserve to get it good and hard." It may be unreasonable, then, to hope that our public officials be more intelligent, honest, or concerned than we the "common people." After all, the pursuit of high office and its trappings of power and privilege is, as the quotes in this book reveal, an exercise engaged in by people more "normal" or "simple" than we would prefer to believe. We must recognize at last that the march of political leadership is a march of all too familiar mediocrities—a March of Follies.

Acknowledgments

I wish to thank the staff of John Wiley & Sons, Inc. for their assistance in making this book possible; and to acknowledge the generosity of Edwin O'Dacre and *The Globe and Mail* for granting me a leave of absence to complete the work. In particular, I am obliged to cite Richard Nixon, J. Danforth Quayle, and my editor, Steve Ross—not necessarily in that order—as sources of inspiration.

• 1 •

On the Campaign Trail

If you would know the depth of meanness of human nature, you have got to be a prime minister running a general election.

JOHN A. MACDONALD, *Canada's first prime minister* (1867)

I think the American public wants a solemn ass as President and I think I'll go along with them.

CALVIN COOLIDGE

A chicken in every pot and two cars in every garage.

Official slogan of HERBERT HOOVER's *successful campaign for the presidency in 1928. The reporter who coined the slogan for the GOP went broke early in the Depression and resorted to begging for loans to support his three children.*

I not only "don't choose to run" but I don't even want to leave a loophole in case I am drafted, so I won't "choose." I will say "won't run" no matter how bad the country will need a comedian at that time.

> WILL ROGERS *in 1931, echoing Calvin Coolidge's statement, "I do not choose to run for president in 1928."*

Arthur, after you have once ridden behind a motorcycle escort, you are never the same again.

> HERBERT H. LEHMAN, *investment banker turned Democratic politician, in 1950, explaining to his brother why he would want to seek a second term as senator from New York after serving four terms as governor of the state*

I don't want my brother to get mixed up with politicians.

> ROBERT KENNEDY, *manager of brother John F. Kennedy's first campaign for a senate seat in 1952, banishing old-time ward heelers from the campaign in favor of Kennedy loyalists drawn from JFK's family and college buddies*

The hardest thing about any political campaign is how to win without proving that you are unworthy of winning.

> ADLAI STEVENSON *in 1952, during his unsuccessful presidential campaign against Dwight Eisenhower*

If the Republicans stop telling lies about us, we will stop telling the truth about them.

ADLAI STEVENSON *in 1952*

---◆---

All parties die at last of swallowing their own lies.
Attributed to JOHN ARBUTHNOT

If you give me a week, I might think of one.
President DWIGHT EISENHOWER's *tepid endorsement of Richard Nixon's 1960 bid for the presidency. Ike had been asked at a press conference: "What major decisions of your administration has the Vice President participated in?" In private, Ike was given to say, "Dick just isn't presidential timber."*

Don't buy a single vote more than necessary. I'll be damned if I'm going to pay for a landslide.
Presidential candidate JOHN F. KENNEDY *in 1960, referring to allegations that his father was bankrolling his campaign, and reporting his father's supposed instructions on the use of family funds*

From here on, LBJ means Let's Back Jack.
LYNDON JOHNSON *in 1960. JFK and his running mate loathed each other even before JFK beat Johnson in the 1960 Democratic primaries, and the feeling would intensify during the Kennedy administration.*

The people have spoke—the bastards.

> DICK TUCK, *longtime dirty trickster for Democratic presidential*
> *candidates in the 1950s and 1960s, on his own 1966 loss in a*
> *California state senate race*

Q: Will you give up your Mercedes?
A: Are you talking of the car now, or the girl?
Q: The car.
A: I won't give up either.

> PIERRE TRUDEAU *campaigning in 1968*

♦

Prosperity is necessarily the first theme of a political campaign.
> WOODROW WILSON *in 1912*

I can't give you too many kisses. The press is watching. Perhaps later.

> PIERRE TRUDEAU *campaigning in 1968, to a party worker*

Voice in the crowd: Vive la France!
Trudeau: Si vous voulez. Vive la France, et vive les Anglais, aussi. Et
vive la république des patates frites.
("Long live the French!" "If you like. Long live the French, and long
live the English, as well. And long live the French fries republic.")

> PIERRE TRUDEAU *campaigning in 1968. Trudeau dedicated his public*
> *career to ridiculing the sentiments of Quebec nationalists.*

When style and charisma connote the idea of contriving, of public
relations, I don't buy it at all.

> RICHARD NIXON, *whose 1968 presidential campaign*
> *was run by advertising executives who carefully controlled*
> *his public appearances so that his carefully scripted*
> *"impromptu" speeches were received only by crowds*
> *of adoring Republicans*

He is the President of every place in this country which does
not have a bookstore.

> Columnist MURRAY KEMPTON in 1968, on the
> calculated nativism of Richard Nixon's campaign

You ought to talk to him about saying "Let me make one thing very clear" ten times every show. It's driving people nuts.

> *A producer on one of Nixon's staged "town-hall meetings" in 1968. Roger Ailes, then a top Nixon aide (and in 1992 chief image director for Dan Quayle), replied, "I have . . . Apparently everybody has been telling him about it but he can't stop."*

If you've seen one ghetto area, you've seen them all.

> *Maryland governor* SPIRO AGNEW, *campaigning in 1968 as Richard Nixon's running mate on the GOP presidential ticket. During the campaign, Agnew referred to a Nisei reporter as a "fat Jap" and called Poles "Polacks."*

We're doing all right. If we could only get someone to play Hide the Greek.

> ROGER AILES *in 1968, on Nixon's running mate, Spiro Agnew*

Mr. Agnew tells us that we lack a sense of humor. I think he is doing his best to restore it.

> EDMUND MUSKIE *campaigning in 1968 as Hubert Humphrey's presidential running mate*

◆

Politics are usually the executive expression of human immaturity.

> VERA BRITTAIN, 1964

The Democratic candidates are a team of permissive candidates who have a penchant for indulging the disorderly and fawning upon lawbreakers.

Vice President SPIRO AGNEW *in 1970, campaigning on behalf of GOP candidates in congressional and gubernatorial races. With the assistance of White House speechwriters William Safire and Patrick Buchanan, Agnew labeled anti-Vietnam War senators "solons of sellout" and "pampered prodigies," described all Democrats as "nattering nabobs of negativism," "pusillanimous pussyfooters" (the term "pussyfoot" was coined by Theodore Roosevelt), "vicars of vacillation," "troglodytic leftists" and "hopeless, hysterical hypochondriacs of history" informed by "foolish fads of phony intellectualism." Despite the high-powered rhetorical campaign, the GOP suffered a large net loss in congressional seats and governorships—including the failure of White-House-backed George Bush to win a senate race in Texas.*

THE WHITE HOUSE

Washington

August 17, 1971

To: The Staff
From: John Dean

This memorandum addresses the matter of how we can maximize the fact of our incumbency in dealing with persons known to be active in their opposition to our Administration. Stated a bit more bluntly—how we can use the available federal machinery to screw our political enemies.

> *A memo that surfaced years later during the Watergate investigations. Dean was a special counsel to the president at the time. The memo, which inspired the creation of a White House "enemies list," a dirty tricks campaign directed at potential Democratic rivals to Nixon in the upcoming election, and a wiretapping operation to uncover the source of White House leaks (the "plumbers unit"), was an indication of how greatly the Nixon team feared losing the presidency in 1972—probably to Edmund Muskie, who in 1970–71 outpolled Nixon in popularity.*

◆

The Presidency, so fought for by fugitives from the sewers.

H. L. MENCKEN *in 1920*

I don't know. I've never played a governor.

> RONALD REAGAN *in 1966, responding to a reporter's question while he was campaigning for California governor: "What kind of governor would you be?"*

Watch what we do, not what we say.

> JOHN MITCHELL, *attorney general in the Nixon administration and head of Nixon's 1972 reelection campaign, to a group of southern black leaders*

An exciting party should have both blondes and brunettes.

>PIERRE TRUDEAU *in 1968, the year he became prime minister of Canada. By "party," Trudeau left unclear whether he was referring to festive gatherings or political organizations.*

I'm gonna be so tough as mayor I'm gonna make Attila the Hun look like a faggot.

>*Philadelphia police commissioner* FRANK RIZZO *during his successful 1971 campaign for mayor*

There is no one sounder in body, mind and spirit than Tom Eagleton.

>*Presidential candidate* GEORGE MCGOVERN *in 1972, defending his running mate, Senator Thomas F. Eagleton, after it was revealed that Eagleton had years earlier received electroshock treatment for depression. Before dumping Eagleton in favor of Sargent Shriver,*

McGovern added that he was "1,000 percent for Tom Eagleton" and had "no intention of dropping him from the ticket." Mort Sahl later said Eagleton's only sin was being depressed before he joined the McGovern team.

I thought the [1972 Democratic] convention was great, but what came across on television, apparently, to many [voters] was they saw a lot of aggressive women, they saw a lot of militant blacks, they saw long-haired kids, and I think that combination, which helped win the [Democratic presidential] nomination for me, I think it offended a lot of them.

> GEORGE MCGOVERN *in 1972, reflecting on his loss to Richard Nixon. McGovern could have added that, off-screen, the media saw and was greatly influenced by one of the most hugely disorganized presidential campaigns of this century, run by an arrogant, scruffy-haired young man named Gary Hart.*

◆

Delegates are not the noblest sons and daughters of the Republic; a man of taste, arrived from Mars, would take one look at a convention floor and leave forever, convinced he had seen one of the drearier squats of Hell.

> NORMAN MAILER on the 1960 Democratic National Convention

I've looked on a lot of women with lust. I've committed adultery in my heart many times.

> *Presidential candidate* JIMMY CARTER *in a 1976 interview with* Playboy. *Carter made the comments as the* Playboy *reporters were packing to leave, assuming, incorrectly, that they had shut off their tape recorder.*

There's no Soviet domination of Eastern Europe, and there never will be under a Ford Administration.

> *President* GERALD FORD *in a nationally televised debate with Jimmy Carter in 1976, doing his best to help voters forget Carter's musing on adultery*

Q: Generally speaking, are you satisfied that you have done a thorough enough job of checking your basic [speaking] material?

A: Yes, I do. I've been on the mashed potato circuit for a great many years, probably a quarter of a century. And I learned very early that you should check them. I didn't at first, I guess, like any other speaker. I'd see something and think, hey, that's great, and use it. And I just learned from being rebutted a couple of times that I'd better be sure of my facts.

> *Presidential candidate* RONALD REAGAN *in 1980, interviewed by CBS correspondent Bill Plante*

> *The man who can make two ears of corn, or two blades of grass, grow on the spot where only one grew before would deserve better of mankind, and render more essential service to the country, than the whole race of politicians put together.*
>
> JONATHAN SWIFT

If I win, I win. And if I lose, I spare myself untold agony.

JOHN CROSBIE, *unsuccessful candidate for the Progressive Conservative Party leadership in 1983 (he lost to Brian Mulroney)*

After I've been prime minister for 15 years and I can't find a living, breathing Tory in the country.

BRIAN MULRONEY, *campaigning for the leadership of the Progressive Conservative Party in 1983, promising party faithful that there will be plenty of patronage jobs for rival Liberals and New Democrats—eventually*

I was my best successor but I decided not to succeed myself.

PIERRE TRUDEAU *in 1984, announcing he would not lead his party into the next general election*

Gary Hart, campaigning for the Democratic nomination for the presidency in 1984:

She [his wife, Lee] campaigns in California and I campaign in New Jersey.

Lee: I got to hold a koala bear.

Gary: I won't tell you what I got to hold. Samples of a toxic waste dump.

> GARY HART, *three days after this exchange at a Los Angeles fundraiser, tries to make amends with New Jersey voters, saying, "The people of New Jersey are more intelligent than that. They know a remark made in jest and lightheartedly . . . was not meant disparagingly about this state." Hart wins the California primary but loses New Jersey to Walter Mondale.*

◆

The second law, Rakove's law of principle and politics, states that the citizen is influenced by principle in direct proportion to his distance from the political situation.

MILTON RAKOVE, in *Virginia Quarterly Review*, 1965

Let's face it, there's no whore like an old whore. If I'd been in Bryce's position I'd have been right in there with my nose in the public trough like the rest of them. . . . I hope this is all off the record. I'm taking the high road now.

> BRIAN MULRONEY *in 1984, campaigning for prime minister of Canada, telling reporters on his campaign plane that he could*

sympathize with recent patronage appointee Bryce Mackasey. Criticism of the Mackasey appointment and several other patronage abuses was the central platform of Mulroney's campaign.

He reminds every American woman of her first husband.
> ART BUCHWALD *in 1986, on the campaigning style of Vice President George Bush as he stumped for GOP candidates in the 1986 "off-year" elections*

Now, the simple truth is those Democrats who are here are probably here because like millions I've met across the country, they have found they can no longer follow the leadership of the Republican Party, which has taken them down a course that leads to ruin.
> *President* RONALD REAGAN *in 1986, campaigning on behalf of Republican Senate candidate Jim Santini*

—————————————— ◆ ——————————————

To govern mankind one must not overrate them.
> LORD CHESTERFIELD

Style is substance.
> WILLIAM VANDER ZALM, *unapologetic about the lack of policy in his campaign, on the eve of winning the biggest victory of any premier in British Columbia history, in 1986*

Follow me around. I don't care. I'm serious. If anybody wants to put a tail on me, go ahead. They'd be very bored.

Democratic presidential candidate GARY HART *in April 1987. The* Miami Herald, *taking him up on his offer, staked out Hart's Washington townhouse and reported on May 3 that he had spent a night there with Donna Rice.*

---◆---

Congressional investigations are for the benefit of photographers.

WILL ROGERS

I can't wait. It's blood lust. Let me at him. I hate him. I hate all of them. I think they're the phoniest two-bit bastards that ever came down the pike. They are just a [expletive] bunch of meddlesome bastards.

BILL CARRICK, *campaign manager for Democratic presidential candidate Richard Gephardt, on Democratic nomination rivals Albert Gore and his aides, in 1988*

If I didn't like Senator Dole, I'd say he's being deceptive. But I do like him, so I'll just say he's waffling.

JOHN SUNUNU, *spearheading George Bush's successful bid to win the New Hampshire primary in 1988, on his allegation that Bush rival Robert Dole had been inconsistent in his position on a possible oil-import fee*

Stop lying about my record!

> ROBERT DOLE *in 1988, debating presidential rival George Bush on*
> *live TV*

Al Capone said, "We don't want no trouble," and that's how the Democratic Party feels. They want to play it safe. That's how they got Walter Mondale, and that's how they'll end up with Michael Dukakis.

> *Presidential candidate* GARY HART *in 1988*

Heal.

> *Presidential candidate* JESSE JACKSON, *laying hands on the forehead of*
> *former Texas governor John Connally, a Democrat-turned-*
> *Republican, in 1988*

George Bush has met more heads of foreign states than I have. But a substantial number of them were dead.

> JESSE JACKSON *in 1988, referring to Vice President George Bush's*
> *dutiful appearance at state funerals*

I was the only [candidate] born in Stonewall Jackson's birthplace. I'm the only one who went to the school where Robert E. Lee was president.

> PAT ROBERTSON, *reviewing his qualifications for the presidency while*
> *campaigning in South Carolina in 1988*

He's chickening out of the trial just like he chickened out 37 years ago.

> Former congressman PETE MCCLOSKEY on Pat Robertson's decision
> to drop a libel suit against him over comments about Robertson's
> service record in the Korean War

The House [of Representatives] looks like more fun. It's like the "Donahue" show. The Senate is like one of those Sunday morning public-service programs.

> Talk-show host PHIL DONAHUE, musing about his "50–50" likelihood
> of running for political office in 1988

That was the ultimate heckle.

> Presidential candidate ALBERT GORE, responding to a
> university student who yelled that Gore would make a good vice
> president, in 1988

I feel a little like Zsa Zsa Gabor's fifth husband. I know what I'm supposed to do but I'm not sure I know how to make it interesting.

> Senator ALBERT GORE in 1988, on following 23 previous speakers at
> a Democratic Party function

In the last two elections, with two whites on the ticket, we lost 49 of 50 states. We can't do much worse than that.

> Ohio Democratic Representative LOUIS STOKES in 1988, on the
> likely outcome for the Democrats with Jesse Jackson on the
> presidential ticket

You've got to get your ass out of that Kenny-buck-port or whatever its name is, board it up and get down to Texas.

Texas governor BILL CLEMENTS *in 1988, warning GOP presidential candidate George Bush to make the acquaintance of Texas voters*

If you told him to bunt, he bunted.

Endorsement of George Bush in 1988 by his Yale baseball coach,
ETHAN ALLEN, *age 86*

Poor George is hopelessly inarticulate. He never finishes a sentence or puts in a verb.

Endorsement of George Bush by sister NANCY ELLIS

I think George would be marvelous with the poor. . . . I didn't mean to say he'd be as dedicated as, say, Ted Kennedy. But, really, he'd be marvelous.

Endorsement of George Bush by sister NANCY ELLIS

God help us from people who think they are going around exercising their goodness.

Endorsement of George Bush by cousin RAY WALKER, *who didn't buy the "kinder, gentler" message*

[You're] talking about yourself too much.

Advice to George Bush from his mother DOROTHY BUSH *during the 1988 campaign*

That's the funniest line of the convention.

> *Former senator* GARY HART *in 1988 to actress Morgan Fairchild,*
> *who introduced herself to him, saying, "We met once before. I don't*
> *know if you remember me."*

It wasn't my finest hour. It wasn't even my finest hour and a half.

> *Arkansas governor* BILL CLINTON *on his numbingly long and dull*
> *nomination speech for Michael Dukakis at the 1988 Democratic*
> *National Convention*

How do we make equality of opportunity a reality in America?
We can start by supporting the equal-rights amendment, and I
support the REA.

> *Senator* LLOYD BENTSEN, *Michael Dukakis's running mate, in*
> *1988 to the National Federation of Business and Professional*
> *Women's Clubs. He was referring to the ill-fated Equal Rights*
> *Amendment (ERA).*

I can't answer in that context.

> *President* RONALD REAGAN'S *tepid endorsement of George Bush's bid*
> *for the presidency, when asked in 1988 to give an example of Bush's*
> *input on White House policy decisions*

I'm going to have to arrive at that if there are no others.

> *President* RONALD REAGAN *in May 1988, still managing to restrain*
> *his enthusiasm for the Bush candidacy*

You know, if I listened to him long enough, I would be convinced we're in an economic downturn and people are homeless and going without food and medical attention and that we've got to do something about the unemployed.

President RONALD REAGAN *in 1988, on Democratic presidential candidate Michael Dukakis*

◆

The men the American people admire most extravagantly are the most daring liars; the men they detest most violently are those who try to tell them the truth. A Galileo could no more be elected President of the United States than he could be elected Pope of Rome. Both high posts are reserved for men favored by God with an extraordinary genius for swathing the bitter facts of life in bandages of soft illusion.

H. L. MENCKEN in 1918

Look, I'm not going to pick on an invalid.

President RONALD REAGAN *in 1988, asked if Democratic presidential candidate Michael Dukakis should release his medical records. Twenty minutes later, Reagan said, "I think I was kidding, but I don't think I should have said what I said."*

You've said many times in this campaign that you want to give America back to the little guy. Mister Vice President, I am that man.

Diminutive presidential candidate MICHAEL DUKAKIS *to George Bush at the 1988 Alfred E. Smith Memorial Dinner*

---------------------------- ♦ ----------------------------

*Offices are as acceptable here as elsewhere, and whenever a
man has cast a longing eye on them, a rottenness begins in
his conduct.*

THOMAS JEFFERSON, in a letter to Tench Coxe, 1799

I remember I was very sweet on Janet Leigh for a while, but I think
that was mostly physical.

Presidential candidate MICHAEL DUKAKIS *in 1988, when asked to
name his favorite movie stars*

I knew Jack Kennedy. Jack Kennedy was my friend. You're no
Jack Kennedy.

Senator LLOYD BENTSEN *takes issue during a nationally televised
debate with Dan Quayle's assertion of his own Kennedylike attributes*

[I have] more skeletons in my closet than the Smithsonian.

BEN JONES, *a former alcoholic once charged with battery
against his ex-wife, who played Cooter in the TV
series "Dukes of Hazzard," in 1988. Jones, a
Georgia Democrat, won a congressional race against
incumbent Pat Swindall, who at the time faced a
perjury indictment over his role in a money-laundering
scheme involving a loan for his home.*

I think I could bring some new blood to the office.

> *Campaign slogan of* MIKE PULLIAM, *who lost his 1988 bid for coroner of Hughes County, South Dakota*

I just wasn't able to convince voters that "Dukakis" was Greek for "Bubba."

> LLOYD BENTSEN *soon after the 1988 election, explaining why the Democrats didn't carry Bentsen's home state of Texas*

You just pointed your finger and emphasized the problem we're trying to resolve.

> *Texas gubernatorial candidate* JACK RAINS *in 1989, after a reporter objected that his ten-point education reform plan had only nine points*

We need fewer farmers at this point in time.
> *Republican senator* DAVID K. KARNES *of farm-state Nebraska,*
> *speaking at the Nebraska State Fair in 1988 in an election campaign*
> *he was destined to lose to former Nebraska governor Robert Kerrey*

The party of homosexuals.
> *Utah senator* ORRIN HATCH *in 1988, describing the Democrats at a*
> *Republican fund-raiser*

◆

In the United States today it is almost inconceivable what kind
of rubbish a public man must utter if he is to keep respectable.
> JOHN MAYNARD KEYNES *in 1932*

How did you like my courageous silence on abortion?
> BRIAN MULRONEY *to an aide after a televised debate in 1988 in which*
> *he had ducked the abortion issue*

You don't need brains for this job, just physical stamina.
> AUDREY MCLAUGHLIN, *hours before winning the leadership of*
> *Canada's New Democratic Party in 1989*

I stay in enough trouble when I'm sober.
> *Arkansas gubernatorial candidate* TOMMY ROBINSON *in 1990, when*
> *asked about rumors that he used to drink a pint of bourbon a day*

I neither want [to be] nor am a holier-than-thou. I've seen about everything, heard just about everything and done part of it.

> *Senator* JESSE HELMS, *crusader for prudery in art, campaigning for reelection in 1990*

I think it proves that North Carolina doesn't want a senator who knows how to cuss.

> BO THOMAS, *in 1990, on losing the Democratic primary for the North Carolina senate*

Only a governor can make executions happen. I did. And I will.

> *Former Texas governor* MARK WHITE *in 1990, campaigning for reelection*

Hal was an effective commissioner right up to the end and beyond.

> *Cook County (Ill.) commissioner* CARL HANSEN *in 1990, on fellow commissioner Harold Tyrell, who won reelection despite the fact he is dead*

◆

Anyone who deliberately tries to get himself elected to a public office is permanently disqualified from holding one.

> SIR THOMAS MORE, *Utopia*

I wonder if they'll vote for a dead man.

> BILL CLINTON *in 1992, reflecting sourly on the travails of seeking public office while fighting off a cold and allergies during a week of campaigning in New Hampshire*

The words and phrases are powerful. Read them. Memorize as many as possible. And remember that like any tool, these words will not help if they are not used.

> *Instructions in a manual distributed during the 1990 election season by Gopac, an elision of GOP and PAC (for political action committee). A cover letter accompanying the glossary of adjectives, entitled "Language, a Key Mechanism of Control," was signed by Gopac's general chairman, Republican congressman Newt Gingrich of Georgia. GOP candidates are advised by the manual to label their opponent a "sick, pathetic, liberal, incompetent tax-spending traitor." Other terms for use include decay, unionized bureaucracy, greed, corruption, radical, permissive, and bizarre. GOP hopefuls are instructed to refer to themselves as a "humane, visionary, confident, candid, hard-working reformer," and to apply to their own platforms such terms as opportunity, challenge, courage, pristine, principle(d), care(ing), common sense, peace, and pioneer. Gopac executive director Kay Riddle, asked by reporters about the 113-word glossary, said, "Traitor was inadvertently used. It was in no way meant to imply patriotism or lack of patriotism. When we do use it, we would mean it more as traitor to the [congressional] district, someone elected as a moderate who became a liberal."*

[It's] been an unexciting and dull campaign. With me in it, it's no longer dull.

Ohio congressman BUZ LUKENS, *convicted of having sex with a minor, on his 1990 decision to seek reelection*

Our United States Senate is just chock full of song-and-dance men—62 of them. They are called lawyers and David (Porky) Boren is one of them. Isn't there room in this exclusive club of male clowns for a real honest-to-goodness clown?

Oklahoma senate candidate VIRGINIA JENNER *in 1990, on why she wore a clown suit while campaigning against Senator David Boren*

Well, I will tell you something about that area. There is no point in my making a speech on crime control to a bunch of addicts.

Massachusetts gubernatorial candidate JOHN SILBER *in 1990, on why he chose not to announce his crime-control platform in a mostly African-American neighborhood in Boston*

When you've had a long life and you're ripe, then it's time to go.

JOHN SILBER, 63, *explaining why he favors rationing of health benefits for the elderly*

Maine is a good location for a nuclear power plant—where the damn thing could have an accident and not hurt anybody.

JOHN SILBER *in 1990, during his unsuccessful bid to become Massachusetts governor*

I feel a great kinship to him.

> *Texas gubernatorial candidate* JIM MATTOX *in 1990, comparing himself to Jesus Christ*

If it's inevitable, just lay back and enjoy it.

> CLAYTON WILLIAMS *at a rained-out campaign event during the 1990 gubernatorial race in Texas. Williams, who lost to Ann Richards, was advising reporters at the event to compare the weather with how one should cope with rape.*

I've noticed that nothing I never said has hurt me.
> CALVIN COOLIDGE

I always thought [Himmler] was one of the toughest campaigners, but what Ann Richards has done would make Himmler blush.

> *Former Texas gubernatorial candidate* MARK WHITE *in 1990, attributing his loss to Richards in the state primary to her anti-White commercials*

You allow me to license and regulate marijuana, and I'll fill every hotel and motel room in the state of Kentucky.

> GATEWOOD GALBRAITH, *Democratic gubernatorial candidate, on his campaign platform of legalizing pot in order to boost tourism, in 1991*

---◆---

Politicians are the same all over. They promise to build bridges, even where there are no rivers.

NIKITA KHRUSHCHEV in 1960, at a Long Island, New York press conference

---

I believe in the natural family order where the man works and the woman stays home and raises the kids. It's what the people want and what they will get if I am elected governor.

LARRY FORGY, *Republican candidate for governor of Kentucky, in 1991*

The bad news is that one-third of the people think I'm the banker who foreclosed on their farm, one-third think I run the oil company that raised the price of gasoline and one-third think I'm the guy who sold Manhattan to the Japanese.

Senator JAY ROCKEFELLER, *short-lived candidate for the Democratic presidential nomination in 1991, explaining the drawbacks of having "100 percent" name recognition in Iowa*

It was an insensitive, stupid joke told by, hopefully, a temporarily stupid politician.

Nebraska senator ROBERT KERREY, *candidate for the Democratic presidential nomination, apologizing in 1991 for telling a lesbian joke to another candidate in what he thought was a private conversation*

The good news is that the lesbians are upset with Kerrey. The bad news is that they'll be coming our way to support us.

> DAVID BECKWITH, *Dan Quayle's press secretary, in 1991*

The average guy is not on the golf course, the tennis court, or a speedboat because he doesn't have one.

> RICHARD NIXON *in 1991, reportedly warning George Bush and Dan Quayle that their recreational habits could cost them votes*

That's his name. Mario, Mario, Mario, Mario, Mario, Mario. He better get used to it.

> *White House spokesman* MARLIN FITZWATER *in 1991, responding to Mario Cuomo's suggestion that Dan Quayle called him Mario to cast aspersions on his Italian background*

It's hard when you have to choose between a crook and a Nazi.

> *Former Louisiana governor* DAVID TREEN *summing up the choices facing electors in the 1991 gubernatorial race in which former Ku Klux Klan leader David Duke won a majority of white votes but lost the election to twice-indicted, never-convicted, former governor Edwin Edwards*

One person described me as the Boris Yeltsin of American politics. I like that.

> DAVID DUKE *in 1991, campaigning in the Louisiana gubernatorial race*

Between Tom Campbell and Sonny Bono, they have the bad-haircut vote sewn up.

> JOE GELMAN, *advisor to California Republican state*
> *senate candidate Bruce Herschensohn, on the*
> *Republican primary opponents, in 1991*

Do I have any foreign-policy experience? No. Did I have any experience before writing a song? No. Producing a show? No. Running for mayor? No.

> SONNY BONO, *mayor of Palm Springs, California, after announcing*
> *his candidacy for the Senate in 1991*

You are neither hot nor cold so I vomited you out of my mouth. That's what I say about moderates.

> *Presidential candidate* JERRY BROWN *in 1991, referring*
> *to what he considers to be strident liberalism among*
> *his Democratic rivals*

♦

Being a politician is like being a football coach. You have to be
smart enough to understand the game, but dumb enough to
think it's important.

EUGENE MCCARTHY

I think God made all people good. But if we had to take a million immigrants in, say, Zulus next year, or Englishmen, and put them in Virginia, what group would be easier to assimilate and would cause less problems for the people of Virginia?

Presidential candidate PATRICK BUCHANAN *in 1991, advocating a "Buchanan fence"—a trench along the Mexican border to control illegal immigration*

When the crazies called [with offers to support Richard Nixon's 1968 presidential bid] I automatically handed them over to Pat. Attila the Hun? Oh, you want to speak to Buchanan.

Former Nixon aide JOHN SEARS *in 1992, endorsing his former coworker on the Nixon team. The reference is to Buchanan's combative rhetorical style.*

I am in Washington, not of it. No insider challenges an incumbent president. That makes me, de facto, an outsider.

Presidential candidate PATRICK BUCHANAN *in 1992, responding on the TV program "Crossfire" to his former "Crossfire" cohost Michael Kinsley's question: "You've lived here [in Washington] all your life. You've either been in the media or the government. You never had an honest job in your life and you've never run anything in your life. What makes you qualified to be president and run the whole country and makes you qualified to portray yourself as some sort of outsider populist?" Buchanan, a native of Washington and a speechwriter in the Nixon, Ford, and Reagan administrations, lives so close to the CIA's headquarters in suburban Virginia, The New York Times' Maureen Dowd reported, that his cat keeps setting off the security sensors buried in the woods around the agency complex.*

Pat's going to win. I'm going to see to it. I don't care where I have to break in.

> G. GORDON LIDDY, *Watergate conspirator, endorsing the Buchanan candidacy in 1991*

My, that's got every fire hydrant in America worried.

> *Presidential candidate* BILL CLINTON *in 1992, on hearing that Vice President Dan Quayle had declared his intention to be a "pit bull" in helping the GOP retain the White House in the fall election*

Isn't that a little like calling Moe the most intelligent of the Three Stooges?

> BILL CLINTON'*s response after being introduced to a New Hampshire speakers' forum in 1991 as the smartest of the candidates seeking the Democratic presidential nomination*

◆

I always wanted to get into politics, but I was never light enough to make the team.

ART BUCHWALD

Let's try winning and see what it feels like. If we don't like it, we can go back to our traditions.

> *Democratic presidential candidate* PAUL TSONGAS *in 1991*

Patience. Patience. I'll catch up. My strategy is to peak on election day.

> *Presidential candidate* TOM HARKIN, *reassuring supporters in 1992*

When I was in England, I experimented with marijuana a time or two, and I didn't like it, and I didn't inhale, and I never tried it again.

> BILL CLINTON *in March 1992, uttering what* The New Republic *termed "his least believable campaign statement to date." New York* Times *columnist Anna Quindlen called Clinton's claim "the equivalent of saying that you drank a beer, but didn't swallow."*

My doctor ordered me to shut up, which will make the American people happy.

> BILL CLINTON *in April 1992, after being told by his physician to rest his sore larynx*

The SuperMario Noncandidacies

We see our mission to be the completion of the work of Creation.
> *New York governor* MARIO CUOMO *on the ambition that drove him to seek public office*

Even with Sherman, I could think of ways to get around it. All you'd have to say to him is, "General, have you ever changed your mind?"
> MARIO CUOMO *in 1988, on the difficulty of making clear his presidential ambitions. In a message to the 1884 Republican National Convention, General William Tecumseh Sherman wrote, "I will not accept if nominated and will not serve if elected."*

In *Waiting for Godot*, the whole point is that Godot never shows up.
> MARIO CUOMO *explaining his noncandidacy in 1988*

We don't have to do what the candidates do—talk about huge issues in 30 seconds in a field somewhere, trying to make sure cows don't urinate on our shoes.
> MARIO CUOMO *in 1988, suggesting a motive for why he, Sam Nunn, and Bill Bradley had opted not to seek the presidency*

I endorse him! I endorse him! I endorse him! There, three times I endorsed him.
> MARIO CUOMO, *pressed once too often about his tepid endorsement of Michael Dukakis's presidential bid in 1988*

If you had asked me if there were a possibility of having an earthquake and a typhoon while I was visiting Japan, I would have said it was not likely. But since I arrived there has been an earthquake and a typhoon.

> MARIO CUOMO *in Japan, where questions about a renewed Cuomo noncandidacy for the 1992 election season were raised by reporters*

I'm trying to decide between the King David and the White House.

> MARIO CUOMO *in 1990, explaining his future plans to a resident of the King David Manor nursing home in Long Beach, New York*

I have no plans, and no plans to make plans.

> MARIO CUOMO *in 1990, deferring the Big Decision*

They said, "Will you think about it?" I said, "Sure, I'll think about it. I'm always thinking about it." I said I'd have to be mindless not to think about it. I don't talk about it, but I think about it. Of course I do.

> MARIO CUOMO *in 1991, keeping hopes of a Cuomo candidacy burning bright*

It is easier to appear worthy of a position one does not hold, than of the office which one fills.

LA ROCHEFOUCAULD

This field is adequate to produce the next President of the United States.

> Mario Cuomo *in February 1992, two months after declaring he would not be a candidate for the presidency, damning with faint praise the field of Democratic contenders for Bush's job*

We're getting letters—I just asked them [his aides]. Did you hear about the letters we got? How many letters did we get? Anybody know? Ten thousand?

> Mario Cuomo *at a 1992 press conference, where he was asked to comment on the plight of a New Hampshire man whose telephone number is similar to that of a Cuomo write-in campaign committee. Instead of responding to the question about the inconvenience suffered by this man Cuomo launched into a rambling discussion about the many letters and calls to his office encouraging him to seek the presidency, and said eight people had been recruited in the Governor's office to handle this flood of supportive messages.*

Only when I'm awake.

> Mario Cuomo *in February 1992, when asked if he regretted not running*

Would you be willing to say that you'd believe it if I said I was willing to say I wouldn't change my mind?

> Mario Cuomo *in February 1992, on his thoughts about a presidential bid*

What do you want me to say? "Write in Pinocchio, not Mario?"

MARIO CUOMO *in February 1992, on why he refused to criticize a write-in campaign on his behalf in New Hampshire*

The Tex-Prep Campaigns of George Bush

Do I have a mounting confidence that I could lead? You bet. Would I be a good president? . . . I'd be crackerjack!

GEORGE BUSH *campaigning in the 1980 primaries*

◆

The world is weary of statesmen whom democracy has degraded into politicians.

British prime minister BENJAMIN DISRAELI

I mean, like, hasn't everybody thought about becoming president for years?

GEORGE BUSH *campaigning in 1980*

I'm going to be so much better a president for having been at the CIA that you're not going to believe it.

GEORGE BUSH *campaigning in 1980*

A President We Won't Have to Train.

GEORGE BUSH's *1980 campaign slogan*

Gee, what good people Reagan has around him. These guys are really bright. *Really* bright . . . Gosh, a new president can really make a difference.

GEORGE BUSH *at the 1980 Republican National Convention lobbying for a spot on the GOP ticket next to presidential nominee Ronald Reagan*

If this doesn't work out, I'm gonna be the pissedest-off guy around.

GEORGE BUSH *at the GOP convention, speculating on the outcome of his veep-spot lobbying efforts*

Do you know what wins elections? It's who puts money into this and who takes money out.

Vice President GEORGE BUSH *campaigning for reelection in 1984. He could have been talking about the evil taxmen or the evil PAC-men; one couldn't tell, except that he was waving a wallet in the air.*

◆

As long as I count the votes what are you going to do about it? Say.

WILLIAM M. "BOSS" TWEED

It looks like Edith and Archie have turned out to be Pamela and Averell Harriman, *dahling.*

> GEORGE BUSH *commenting on the disclosure of personal finances by 1984 vice-presidential rival Geraldine Ferraro and her husband*

I mean, whine on, harvest moon!

> GEORGE BUSH *during the 1984 televised debate with Geraldine Ferraro, referring to Walter Mondale's pessimism about the nation's future*

There are an awful lot of things I don't remember.

> GEORGE BUSH *in 1984, asked if his credibility is in question for having switched from supporting choice in abortion to opposing it*

Boy, I'm glad that thing's over. I don't need any more of that.

> GEORGE BUSH *moments after the debate with Ferraro was over. In helping Bush prepare for the debate, one of his coaches advised him to "go out there and look like you're enjoying yourself, even if you're not."*

We tried to kick a little ass last night.

> GEORGE BUSH, *recovered from the Ferraro debate, to a dockworker. Realizing the comment had probably been picked up by a boom microphone, Bush said, "Whoops. Oh, God, he heard me. Turn that thing off." In a subsequent press conference, Bush characterized the remark as merely "an old Texas football expression."*

To hear these guys wringing their hands about everything being wrong with this country, I'm sorry, I just am all depressed, want to switch over to see "Jake and the Fatman" on CBS.

> GEORGE BUSH *in 1987, asked for his reaction to an NBC candidates' debate among Democratic presidential hopefuls*

There are things we can do to give us a little more attention. . . . I've got to look more frantic.

> GEORGE BUSH *in 1987, speaking to campaign aides*

Finis!!!

> GEORGE BUSH *in 1988, while ripping a flyer published by GOP rival Jack Kemp from a teenage girl's hands and tearing it up*

[**T**hey were] at their daughters' coming-out parties, or teeing up at the golf course for that all-important last round.

> GEORGE BUSH's *deadpan explanation for his third-place finish in the Iowa caucuses in 1988, suggesting that his core supporters were otherwise occupied. Bush's damage-control center put out the word that their man had been joking about the sort of people who were likely to vote for him.*

A recent poll tells why the people of New Hampshire are supporting George Bush. Forty percent like my foreign policy. Forty percent support my economic policy. And 20 percent believe I make a good premium beer.

GEORGE BUSH *campaigning in New Hampshire in 1988*

If this country . . . ever loses its interest in fishing, we got real trouble.

GEORGE BUSH *during the 1988 primaries*

I'd tell you "Hee-Haw," but you wouldn't believe it, and it's not on any more anyway.

GEORGE BUSH *in 1988, when asked what TV shows he likes*

You've seen the portraits of the Mayflower. My people are the ones waving Bloomingdale's shopping bags.

GEORGE BUSH *at the annual Alfred E. Smith Memorial Dinner in New York in 1988*

Liberals feel unworthy of their possessions. Conservatives feel they deserve everything they've stolen.

MORT SAHL

Watch my vice-presidential decision. That will tell all.

> GEORGE BUSH *in 1988, responding to critics who said he had yet to define what he stood for*

I hope I stand for antibigotry, anti-Semitism, antiracism. That is what drives me.

> GEORGE BUSH *in 1988, attempting to distance himself from eight campaign aides who resigned over allegations of engaging in anti-Semitic activities. Mario Cuomo remarked that Bush at least had not offended Italians by declaring himself antipasto.*

He will go down in my book as *the* great governor of the State of California.

> GEORGE BUSH *in 1988, referring to outgoing governor George Deukmejian, and clearing up the mystery behind former California governor Ronald Reagan's tepid support of Bush's presidential bid*

I want to try to keep it that I don't go out and do something to tear down and be negative about the president. It may not always be that easy.

> GEORGE BUSH *in 1988, on his strategy for dealing with questions about his role in the Reagan administration*

We have had triumphs, we have made mistakes, we have had sex.

> GEORGE BUSH *campaigning in Twin Falls, Idaho, during the 1988 presidential race, accompanied on this occasion by Ronald Reagan. Bush, speaking of his eight years as Vice President under Reagan, meant to say "we have had setbacks."*

[**Y**ou'll be able to] send your college to children.
> GEORGE BUSH *in 1988, explaining how he will make a difference as*
> *"the education president"*

[**Y**ou] don't have to go to college to achieve success. We need the people who do the hard physical work of our society.
> GEORGE BUSH, *education-president-in-waiting, during a 1988 talk*
> *with Hispanic high school students in East Los Angeles*

We could use that kind of ability.
> GEORGE BUSH *in 1988, offending U.S. autoworkers by joking that*
> *mechanics from the Soviet Union should be brought to Detroit to help*
> *bolster the nation's industrial prowess*

They always bring 'em by me. I say to them, "Be sure I look at it."
> GEORGE BUSH *in 1988, explaining his policy on quotes written for*
> *him by his staff*

That's what I intend.
> GEORGE BUSH *in 1988, when asked about his unclear stand*
> *regarding conflict-of-interest allegations directed at White House aide*
> *Edwin Meese*

Make that 10.
> GEORGE BUSH *in 1988, after being corrected by wife Barbara on the*
> *number of his grandchildren*

I'll try to hold my charisma in check.

GEORGE BUSH *in 1988*

What's wrong with being a boring kind of guy? . . . I think to kind of suddenly try to get my hair colored, dance up and down in a miniskirt or do something to show I've got a lot of jazz out there and drop a bunch of one-liners . . . we're talking about the president of the United States. This is serious business . . . I kind of think I'm a scintillating kind of fellow.

GEORGE BUSH *in 1988*

I know inside I've got a lot of fiber here.

GEORGE BUSH *in 1988*

I have a tendency to go on and on and on, but please don't take that for lack of passion. . . . I don't talk much, but I believe. I may not articulate much, but I feel. And my work isn't done yet.

GEORGE BUSH *in 1988*

[He] makes Lesley Stahl look like a pussy.

GEORGE BUSH *in 1988 after being interviewed by Dan Rather*

I want to be positioned in that I could not possibly support David Duke because of the racism and because of the . . . bigotry and all that.

GEORGE BUSH *in 1991, distancing himself from former Klansman David Duke*

Al, you gonna have a draft?

> GEORGE BUSH *on a meet-the-little-people sojourn*
> *(which lasted about 10 minutes) in a dance hall in Beeville,*
> *Texas, in 1991,to companion Alan Simpson.*
> *Senator Simpson ordered a glass of chablis.*

All kinds of weird dances are going on out there.

> GEORGE BUSH *in 1992, apparently referring to the protectionist*
> *stance of Democratic and Republican challengers to his job*

Nitty Ditty Nitty Gritty Great Bird.

> GEORGE BUSH *campaigning in New Hampshire*
> *in January 1992, in an apparent reference to the*
> *Nitty Gritty Dirt Band, whose lyrics he quoted*
> *approvingly in predicting an economic upturn:*
> *"If you want to see a rainbow you've got to*
> *stand a little rain."*

It was one year ago, one year ago that Desert Storm was about—fixin'
to begin, as they say in another of my home states, Texas.

> GEORGE BUSH *in 1992, abruptly shifting into Tex-prep*
> *from English. Bush has variously claimed kinship to*
> *the good people of Massachusetts, where he was*
> *born; to Maine, where his family has long maintained*
> *a summer retreat at Kennebunkport; and to Texas,*
> *where Bush made a small fortune in oil, and which*
> *he briefly represented in Congress.*

So don't feel sorry for—don't cry for me, Argentina. We've got problems . . . and I am blessed by good health.

> GEORGE BUSH *in 1992, waving off sympathy for the ill health he suffered on a state visit to Japan*

♦

> *The office of the President is such a bastardized thing, half royalty and half democracy, that nobody knows whether to genuflect or spit.*
>
> Columnist JIMMY BRESLIN

This ain't the easiest job in the world. . . . Listen, here's the final word. Vote for me. Don't vote for them. Vote for me, okay?

> GEORGE BUSH *in 1992, begging for votes in the New Hampshire primary*

Mrs. Rose Scenario.

> GEORGE BUSH *in New Hampshire in 1992, saying he was trying to look on the bright side of the economy and was searching for "the rainbow out there"*

Somebody said . . . we prayed for you over there [in Japan during his state visit]. That was not just because I threw up on the prime minister of Japan either. Where was He when I needed him? But I said, let me tell you something . . . You cannot be president of the United States if you don't have faith. Remember Lincoln, going to his knees in times of trial in the Civil War and all that stuff. You can't be. And we are blessed.

GEORGE BUSH *in 1992, on the power of faith*

Message: I care.

GEORGE BUSH *in 1992, blurting out verbatim notes prepared by his handlers*

---------------- ◆ ----------------

The most successful politician is he who says what the people are thinking most often in the loudest voice.

THEODORE ROOSEVELT

I'm all for Lawrence Welk. Lawrence Welk is a wonderful man. He used to be or was, or wherever he is now, bless him. But you don't need $700,000 for a Lawrence Welk museum when we've got tough times and people in New Hampshire are hurting.

GEORGE BUSH *campaigning in the New Hampshire primary in February 1992*

Ours is a great state, and we don't like limits of any kind. Ricky Clunn is one of the great bass fishermen. He's a Texas young guy, and he's a very competitive fisherman, and he talked about learning to fish wading in the creeks behind his dad. He in his underwear went wading in the creeks behind his father, and he said—as a fisherman he said it's great to grow up in a country with no limits.

GEORGE BUSH *at a Houston rodeo in February 1992*

This state has gone through hell. It's gone through an extraordinarily difficult time, coming off a pinnacle, you might say, of low unemployment. Now, you're at about the national level. And yes, people are hurting. And I am determined to turn it around. I told some of them over there—there's a big difference, you know. People say to me—difference between domestic and foreign policy. How could you lead the world—and they gave me some credit for that in Desert Storm, that the American people still feel very, very strongly about—and—how can you do that and then have such difficulties with this economy?

Official transcript of a television ad made by
GEORGE BUSH *for use in the New Hampshire primary in February 1992. An astute film editor left most of Bush's comments on the cutting-room floor, with the result that in the finished ad he says simply that, "This state has gone through hell. It's gone through an extraordinarily difficult time." The original version was delivered to a group of insurance workers in Dover, New Hampshire.*

Hey, hey, nihaoma. Hey, yeah, yeah. Heil, heil—a kind of Hitler salute.

> GEORGE BUSH *in March 1992, greeting tourists at Lafayette Park*
> *("Nihaoma" is Cantonese for "How are you?")*

I will say that I think it is enough, and that it's what we ought to do right now—and fight like heck for what we believe in, here. And I think it is.

> GEORGE BUSH *in April 1992, when asked if U.S. policy toward*
> *Russia was belated*

·2·

The Domestic Front

First Days on the Job (Now What?)

I have climbed to the top of the greasy pole.

> BENJAMIN DISRAELI, *British statesman, in 1868, on becoming prime minister*

Well, what do we do now?

> *Newly elected Vice President* GEORGE BUSH *in 1980, to President-elect Ronald Reagan on the day after the election*

Okay, we've won. What do we do now?

> BRIAN MULRONEY *in 1988, moments after learning his party had won reelection*

I am a man of limited talents from a small town. I don't seem to grasp that I am President.

WARREN G. HARDING, *President 1921–1923*

---◆---

Any election is like a horse race, in that you can tell more about it the next day.

JOHN A. MACDONALD

I'm doing it now in the hopes that I will reach the stage like [predecessor] Mackenzie King, where, perhaps after many less years, I'll be able to make all the other people do the work and just go home with my diary.

PIERRE TRUDEAU *in 1969, a year after becoming prime minister of Canada*

I'm a Ford, not a Lincoln.

GERALD FORD *in 1974, upon replacing Richard Nixon as president*

If Lincoln were alive today, he'd roll over in his grave.

Newly inaugurated President GERALD FORD

I guess it just proves that in America anyone can be president.

President GERALD FORD *on his early, gaffe-stricken days in office*

To the young members [of Parliament] who have just come I would say that for the first six months after you are here you will wonder how you got here. Then after that you will wonder how the rest of the members ever got here.

JOHN DIEFENBAKER

You can tell a lot about a fellow's character, if a fellow just picks out one color or grabs a handful.

President-elect RONALD REAGAN *in 1981, on being presented with a jar of jellybeans—his favorite treat while serving in the California governor's mansion—at a Los Angeles farewell gathering*

Does that mean I have to get up?

President-elect RONALD REAGAN *on the morning of January 20, 1981, on being roused from his bed by deputy chief of staff Michael Deaver, who reminded him that today he was "going to be inaugurated"*

When they told me yesterday what had happened, I felt like the moon, the stars and all the planets had fallen on me.

HARRY TRUMAN, telling reporters in 1945 how the news of his ascension to the presidency had affected him

---

Martin came in. He was not radically trying to change things, but then that's about where the parallel ends, because I don't know what he did in his first 100 days.

> President GEORGE BUSH *in 1989, describing his first 100 days in office as being "about the same as Martin Van Buren's"*

The chair's too low.

> DAVID DINKINS *in 1990, recalling his first thoughts after sitting at his desk as mayor of New York*

My first hundred days was saved by those puppy pictures.

> President GEORGE BUSH *in 1989, at the White House News Photographers' Association awards dinner, referring to a recent proliferation of published pictures of the executive mansion's four-legged residents*

The Inner Circle

Look here, McGee, this government can't afford two drunkards—and you've got to stop.

> *Canadian prime minister* JOHN A. MACDONALD,
> *a notorious drinker, to his friend and fellow
> cabinet member D'Arcy McGee at a
> political gathering*

I'm busier than a whore working two beds.

> *Attributed to* C. D. HOWE, *U.S.-born Canadian cabinet minister of
> the 1940s and 1950s*

I've got all my enemies in the cabinet where I can keep an eye on them.

> *Attributed to* JOHN DIEFENBAKER *in 1959, when he was prime
> minister of Canada*

---

*Every time I fill a vacant office I make ten malcontents and
one ingrate.*

LOUIS XIV

I don't see what's wrong with giving Bobby a little experience before he starts to practice law.

> President JOHN F. KENNEDY, *responding to critics who thought Robert Kennedy was a bit young to accept his brother's appointment of him as attorney general*

Hell, anybody can do that job. We've had John Warner.

> President RICHARD NIXON's *low regard for the post of secretary of the Navy. Warner went on to represent Virginia in the senate.*

There are poor people in the cabinet, and there are certainly people in the cabinet that are getting poorer, I can tell you that.

> *Canadian prime minister* PIERRE TRUDEAU *in 1968, a few months after taking office*

If I found in my own ranks that a certain number of guys wanted to cut my throat I'd make sure I cut their throats first.

> PIERRE TRUDEAU

Which one of those idiots would you hire?

> *Former Trudeau cabinet minister* JOHN TURNER, *describing his low estimation of his former colleagues to a Montreal industrialist*

The country is going so far to the right that you won't recognize it.

> JOHN MITCHELL, *attorney general in the Nixon administration, in 1970. The comment, made in a year in which the GOP*

suffered major setbacks in congressional elections, didn't seem
prophetic at the time.

When you have them by the balls, their hearts and minds will soon follow.

Sign posted prominently in the office of CHARLES COLSON, *a top aide in the Nixon administration*

First, a tight pussy; second, loose shoes; and, third, a warm place to shit.

EARL BUTZ, *agriculture secretary in the Ford administration, describing to a friend the three things blacks want. The comment, overheard and reported by Nixon-aide-turned-journalist John Dean, cost Butz his job.*

I am in control.

ALEXANDER HAIG, *secretary of state in the Reagan administration, attempting to calm the nation hours after an attempt had been made on Reagan's life in 1981 by suggesting that he had assumed the powers of the presidential office. Haig lasted only a few more months in the post before being replaced by the more serene George Schultz. Before stepping down, Haig distinguished himself with comments that came to be known as "Haigspeak," and included such expressions as, "I'll have to caveat my response," "posthostage-return attitude," "definitizing an answer," "nuance-al differences" and "This is not an experience I haven't been through before."*

I can't tell until somebody tells me. . . . I never know where I'm going.
RONALD REAGAN *in 1982, when asked if he'd be visiting the Vietnam War Memorial on Veteran's Day*

How are you, Mr. Mayor? I'm glad to meet you. How are things in your city?
President RONALD REAGAN *in 1981, mistaking the only black member of his cabinet, housing secretary Samuel Pierce, during a White House reception for mayors*

We're very proud to have Sugar Ray and Mrs. Ray here.

> *President* RONALD REAGAN *in 1981, welcoming Mr. Leonard and his wife to the White House*

Ed Nitze.

> *President* RONALD REAGAN *in 1983, referring to chief arms negotiator Paul H. Nitze*

I also happen to be someone who believes in tithing—the giving of a tenth.

> *President* RONALD REAGAN *in 1981, a year in which his latest tax returns indicated charitable contributions amounting to 1.4 percent of his income*

We have every kind of mixture you can have. I have a black, I have a woman, two Jews, and a cripple.

> JAMES WATT, *interior secretary in the Reagan administration, describing the composition of an advisory group on coal leasing in 1983. Watt resigned over the comment.*

◆

Washington is a city of southern efficiency and northern charm.

> JOHN F. KENNEDY

I never use the words Democrats and Republicans. It's liberals and Americans.

> JAMES WATT, *interior secretary in the Reagan*
> *administration, in 1982*

What am I supposed to order?
> *President* RONALD REAGAN *in 1984, to an aide while campaigning at*
> *a McDonald's restaurant in Tuscaloosa, Alabama*

If I walked on water people would say I couldn't swim.
> JOHN TURNER, *leader of Canada's Liberal Party, on misgivings about*
> *his abilities expressed by his own partisans*

Otis, what are your thoughts?
> *An "impromptu" comment on one of* RONALD REAGAN's *scripts,*
> *discovered in 1988 by ABC correspondent Sam Donaldson*

Pray for rain.
> *White House spokesman* MARLIN FITZWATER *in 1988, when asked*
> *about the Reagan administration's plans for dealing with a drought*

As we debate these matters, at Exhibition Stadium the Blue Jays are trouncing the Cleveland Indians 9–1 and [Dave] Stieb is pitching a one-hitter.
> GREGORY SORBARA, *Ontario labor minister, responding to a question*
> *about reforming the laws dealing with sexual assault during a*
> *legislature debate in 1988. He apologized for the remark.*

Our cabinet is always unanimous—except when we disagree.
British Columbia premier WILLIAM VANDER ZALM

The Prime Minister's Office is the only bull that travels with its own china shop.
JODI WHITE, *upon retiring in 1988 as chief of staff for the Canadian external affairs ministry*

I'm going to ask—tell them—that I welcome their suggestions as to how Barbara and I can enhance their work. Have a nice house over there, and a lot of ways to hopefully be helpful on that side, from the East Wing side of things.
President GEORGE BUSH *in 1989, giving some idea of his expectations of cabinet officers' input*

I don't care if people hate me, as long as they hate me for the right reasons.
JOHN SUNUNU, *Bush's chief of staff, in 1989 during his first few months in the post. Sununu eventually alienated so many cabinet members that he was forced to resign in late 1991.*

— — — — — — — — — — — ◆ — — — — — — — — — — —

No duty the Executive had to perform was so trying as to put the right man in the right place.
THOMAS JEFFERSON on the art of making government appointments

Treasury secretaries who answer those kinds of questions generally don't last a week after they do—and I like my job.

> NICHOLAS BRADY, *treasury secretary in the Bush administration,*
> *deflecting a 1989 question from a reporter about the value of the*
> *U.S. dollar*

The next time you hear somebody gushing about Woodstock and why can't it be that way today, remind them of the casualty list from Woodstock.

> WILLIAM BENNETT, *antidrug czar in the Bush administration, in*
> *1989. Bennett once went on a blind date with Janis Joplin, a*
> *Woodstock performer who died of a drug overdose.*

There's no moral problem there. I used to teach ethics—trust me.

> WILLIAM BENNETT, *antidrug czar, championing the idea of*
> *decapitating convicted drug dealers in 1989*

I'll sit down with the little spikehead. We'll straighten this thing out.

> WILLIAM BENNETT, *antidrug czar, after criticizing cartoon character*
> *Bart Simpson in 1990. To which the producers of "The Simpsons"*
> *replied, "If our drug czar thinks he can sit down and talk this out with*
> *a cartoon character, he must be on something."*

We don't get any money? Strike whatever I might have said about all that. I didn't know what I was talking about.

> MANUEL LUJAN, *interior secretary in the Bush administration and a*
> *20-year veteran of the House interior committee, after being told by*

an aide during his first major press conference that the government
does not collect royalties from mining rights

An appearance problem.

President GEORGE BUSH *in 1991, brushing aside suggestions that his*
administration had been damaged by John Sununu's weakness for
using government planes, cars, and corporate jets for political
and personal trips

Well, if Quayle does ever ascend to the presidency, you can be sure
he won't fall out of his chair.

JOHN SUNUNU *to an elderly protestor who had taken a bad tumble*
out of his wheelchair after complaining to Sununu about his
extravagant use of government aircraft and about the vice president's
qualifications for office, in 1991

I assure you that in pit bull mode or pussy cat mode (your choice, as
always), I am ready to help.

JOHN SUNUNU *in his 1991 resignation letter to George Bush, not*
so subtly hinting that his strong-arm tactics were once appreciated by
the president

---◆---

The more I see of the representatives of the people, the more I
admire my dogs.

ALPHONSE DE LAMARTINE, 19th-century
French president

I couldn't find a place to land.
JOHN SUNUNU, *shortly before being forced to relinquish his chief-of-staff post, gamely explaining his late arrival at a Washington fund-raiser in 1991*

What's wrong with barbers?
Alberta premier DON GETTY *in 1991, defending the appointment of his barber to the Alberta Gaming Commission*

The Congressional Circus

If you don't want to work for a living this is as good a job as any.
Neophyte congressman JOHN F. KENNEDY *in 1946*

You have to work things out in the cloakroom and when you've got them worked out you can debate a little before you vote.

> *Senate majority leader* LYNDON JOHNSON *on how to make sure congressional deliberations are handled efficiently, if not quite democratically*

This is what Hamlet means by "the insolence of office."

> *Congressman* JOHN F. KENNEDY *to a companion after parking his car in front of a "No Parking" sign in downtown Washington*

It's like a bottle of bourbon. If you take a glass at a time, it's fine. But if you drink the whole bottle in one evening, you have troubles. I plan to take a sip at a time and enjoy myself.

> *President* LYNDON JOHNSON, *fresh from his 1964 landslide victory over Barry Goldwater, alert to the dangers of trying to rush a huge amount of legislation through Congress in the style of FDR's famous first 100 days. The LBJ strategy worked: The former senator got a remarkable 89 bills through the 89th Congress; only two were rejected.*

---- ◆ ----

I never trust a man unless I got his pecker in my pocket.
> LYNDON JOHNSON

Unzip your fly. There's nothing there. John McClellan just cut it off with a razor so sharp you didn't even notice it.

> *President* LYNDON JOHNSON *to domestic policy aide Joseph Califano,*
> *who believed he had negotiated an astute deal with the wily Senator*
> *John McClellan of Arkansas*

Even if he were mediocre, there are a lot of mediocre judges and people and lawyers, and they are entitled to a little representation, aren't they?

> *Republican Senator* ROMAN HRUSKA *of Nebraska in 1970, defending*
> *Richard Nixon's unsuccessful attempt to nominate Harrold Carswell*
> *to the Supreme Court*

The advent of these sleek coaches should provide a tremendous shot in the arm to both legs of Nevada's passenger train system.

> *Senator* HOWARD CANNON *of Nevada in 1980*

Damn it, when you get married, you kind of expect you're going to get a little sex.

> *Alabama Senator* JEREMIAH DENTON, *commenting in 1981 on the*
> *prosecution of a man charged with raping his wife*

———————————————— ◆ ————————————————

Reader, suppose you were an idiot; and suppose you were a member of Congress; but I repeat myself.

MARK TWAIN

Looking ahead, the leadership wishes you a felicific respite from your lucubracations here. May you, after a reposeful holiday, return to these difficile tasks with renewed verve and reviviscent strength.

Democratic whip ROBERT C. BYRD *wishing members of the House of Representatives a happy Easter*

---◆---

There are two periods when Congress does no business: one is before the holidays, and the other after.

GEORGE D. PRENTICE, American journalist

Why you got your boob covered up?

ERNEST KONNYU, *Republican congressman from California, to a 26-year-old female aide. Konnyu later tried to extricate himself from controversy by saying, "At the conference, she wore her name tag . . . right over her boobs. . . . I didn't think it was right for her to have her name tag on in a—it should be up high. She's not exactly heavily stacked, okay? . . . So I told her . . . to move the darn name tag off her boobs." Konnyu was defeated in 1988.*

Dickinson is so poor that they're telling Dickinson jokes in Ethiopia.

North Dakota state representative FRANCIS WALD *in 1988, describing poverty in a region of his state*

Molinari, you creep! Cut out this crap!

> *Senator* ALFONSE D'AMATO *of New York in 1985, not able to believe that the voice on the other end of the phone was that of President Reagan*

There was a time in my life when I spent 90 percent of my money on booze and broads. And the rest of it I just wasted.

> *Neophyte Georgia congressman* BEN JONES, *former star of "The Dukes of Hazzard"*

Do you come here often?

> *Senator* EDWARD KENNEDY *in 1988, to a patron of a Brooklyn soup kitchen*

Capital punishment is our society's recognition of the sanctity of human life.

> *Senator* ORRIN HATCH *of Utah in 1988, advocating the use of the death penalty for murders committed during drug deals*

We didn't do too well with the animal vote, did we? Isn't it the animals who live in these projects? They're not our people.

> *Senator* ALFONSE D'AMATO *of New York, basing his refusal to help find funds for an affordable-housing project in Brooklyn on the paucity of votes he drew there*

       ◆

Fleas can be taught nearly anything that a Congressman can.
MARK TWAIN

Congress would exempt itself from the laws of gravity if it could.
Republican congressman HENRY HYDE *of Illinois, in 1988. Congress is largely exempt from the onerous provisions of, for instance, the Equal Opportunity Act, the Civil Rights Act, the Occupational Safety and Health Act, the Fair Labor Standards Act, and various other pieces of its own legislation imposed on the general public.*

The raise is overdue, there's no question about that.
President and former congressman GEORGE BUSH *during his first press conference in 1989. As he spoke, a GOP fund-raising letter drafted by Lee Atwater was on its way to the party faithful. It read, in part: "There's also a move afoot to let congressmen enjoy yet another whopping pay raise. In this kind of atmosphere, how can President Bush hope to keep your taxes low, cut the budget deficit and keep prosperity growing across the land?"*

I was on federal probation for shooting up mailboxes. I got into a fistfight. I was locked up for disturbing the peace. I was 20 years old. What the hell does that have to do with Al Simpson at 57? What is this crap?
Senator ALAN SIMPSON *of Wyoming in 1989, defending the proposed appointment of John Tower as defense secretary*

 ◆ ---

*Ninety percent of the politicians give the other ten percent a
bad reputation.*

HENRY KISSINGER

You start counting noses on that and we're all dead. You can say that
about anyone, starting with me.

> *Former senator* BARRY GOLDWATER *in 1989, referring to the
> alleged heavy drinking of former senator and defense-secretary
> designate John Tower*

If . . . everybody in this town connected with politics had to leave
town because of [chasing women] and drinking, you'd have no
government.

> *Former senator* BARRY GOLDWATER, *on the Tower candidacy*

I don't know if you know who Barney Frank is, but he's one of the
two members there who are only interested in members of their own
sex. That gives you a little feel for the committee.

> *Republican congressman* CHUCK DOUGLAS *of New Hampshire in
> 1989, charging the House Judiciary Committee with a liberal bias*

We didn't get the pay raise—why work?

> *Senate majority leader* ROBERT DOLE *in 1989, on the slow pace of
> Senate activity*

We've got to do something about the amount of PAC money that goes into congressional campaigns.

Congressman RICHARD GEPHARDT *in 1989, a recipient of more than $600,000 from political action committees in 1987–88*

I know [actor] Don Johnson and he is scum. He's just a long-haired guy with good looks who makes a bundle selling sex, drugs and violence on commercial television.

Senator JAY ROCKEFELLER *of West Virginia in 1989*

Any tree in America would gladly give its life for the glory of a day at home plate.

Congressman DICK DURBIN *in 1989, condemning the trend toward aluminum bats in major league baseball*

Watch out for those tree-planting ceremonies.

Ohio senator JOHN GLENN *in 1989, after being punched by a man mumbling about earthquakes at a Washington, D.C., tree-planting ceremony*

I pledge allegiance to the flag of the United States of America, and to the Republicans for which it stands . . .

Republican congressman BOB MCEWEN *in 1989, opening a day's business in the House with a reference to the GOP's rallying cry in the previous year's elections*

They're always very relieved when Congress is not in session.

> *Senator* DAVID PRYOR *of Arkansas in 1989, returning to Washington after recess, on the mood of his constituents*

I can't think of anything I myself have thought up and written that is all that important.

> *South Carolina congressman* FLOYD SPENCE, *a veteran of the House of Representatives*

I will be grateful for anything you can spare to help me out today.

> *Congressman* BUZ LUKENS *in 1990, convicted of sexual improprieties, in a Christmas-card solicitation for donations*

It could probably be shown by facts and figures that there is no distinctly native American criminal class except Congress.

> MARK TWAIN

When you're sitting in Washington and are from Illinois or New York, you don't get the real picture.

> *Hawaii congresswoman* PATRICIA SAIKI *in 1990, explaining the need for fellow Congress members to flock to her state each winter for their meetings*

Ollie, you've got friends you've never dreamed of. This is from Gerry Studds, the congressman from Massachusetts: *"Hiiiii, sailor."*

> *Congressman* ROBERT DORNAN *in 1990, at a roast for Iran-contra operative Oliver North, reading a fake telegram purportedly written by Studds, who is gay*

I think if they had known I was a member of Congress, I could have understood it.

> *Congressman* GERRY STUDDS *in 1990, after being mugged by two Washington youths*

♦

> *You can't use tact with a Congressman! A Congressman is a hog! You must take a stick and hit him on the snout!*
> U.S. historian HENRY ADAMS, *whose own father and grandfather had been congressmen, in 1906*

This is just my contribution to perestroika.

> *Texas congressman* CHARLIE WILSON *in 1990, when a* Washingtonian *magazine writer saw him inspecting some lace panties with a young Soviet woman in a lingerie shop*

Man, you could make a lot of friends real fast on those subcommittees.

> *Neophyte congressman* JOSEPH KENNEDY II *bucking for membership on the House Energy Committee*

We let our government violate the rights of an old Nazi who is not a criminal.

> *Ohio congressman* JAMES TRAFICANT *in 1990, at an Alabama dinner honoring admitted Nazi Arthur Rudolph, who agreed to leave the United States after charges that he worked Jewish slaves to death during World War II*

Ah-one, ah-two, ah-three, ah-four, ah-half a million dollars.

> *Congressman* SILVIO CONTE, *on the $500,000 in rural-development funds set aside by Congress to promote tourism at the Strasburg, North Dakota, birthplace of Lawrence Welk*

Men should not know how their laws or sausages are made.

OTTO VON BISMARCK

I'm Vanilli because Milli is in the White House.

> *Massachusetts senator* EDWARD KENNEDY *in 1990, who attended his annual Christmas party dressed as a member of the rock act Milli Vanilli, complete with dreadlocks and tights*

You'll hear from 20 senators before you get to speak. It may be the most painful part of the process.

> *Senator* JOSEPH BIDEN, *chairman of the Senate Judiciary Committee, to Supreme Court nominee Clarence Thomas at Thomas's confirmation hearings in 1991*

--- ◆ ---

That one hundred and fifty lawyers should do business together ought not to be expected.

THOMAS JEFFERSON's gloomy outlook regarding the workings of Congress, in his 1821 *Autobiography*

I believe that was the most comprehensive introduction I have ever received. You omitted perhaps one thing—that in 1974 I had a hemorrhoidectomy.

Senator HOWELL HEFLIN *of Alabama, commenting on a lengthy introduction before his address to the American Bankruptcy Institute in 1991*

I come from a state where gun control is just how steady you hold your weapon.

Republican senator ALAN SIMPSON *of Wyoming in 1991*

You're not going to pay by check, are you?

A barber, speaking to Michigan congressman Paul Henry in 1991, a few days after it was revealed via an audit by the General Accounting Office that members of the House of Representatives had bounced a total of 4,325 personal checks at the House bank during the first half of 1990, but the bank had covered them

The Congress has sort of fallen into a pattern of working very hard and taking credit for the speed with which we spin our wheels.

> *Minnesota congressman* VIN WEBER, *on the paltry record of accomplishment of the 102nd Congress, in 1991*

The State Capital Circus

There's nothing wrong with this country that we couldn't cure by turning it over to the police for a couple of weeks.

> *Alabama governor* GEORGE WALLACE *in 1967*

We're going to use every weapon of law enforcement to drive them out of Kent. . . . They're worse than the Brownshirts, and the Communist element and also the night riders and the vigilantes. They're the worst type of people that we harbor in America.

> *Ohio governor* JAMES RHODES *in 1970, ordering National Guardsmen onto the campus of Kent State University to disperse students protesting the Vietnam war. In a short burst of fire, the Guardsmen shot thirteen students, and killed four—none of them protesters, and one a Reserve Officer Training Corps cadet.*

The State of California has no business subsidizing intellectual curiosity.

> RONALD REAGAN *during his first term as California governor, in reference to student unrest on the state's college campuses*

◆
---

*No, no, no, no. You've got it all wrong. Jimmy Stewart for
governor, Ronald Reagan for best friend.*
> Attributed to movie mogul JACK WARNER, Reagan's
> longtime employer, on hearing in 1966 that Reagan
> was running for governor of California

It's our fault. We should have given him better parts.
> JACK WARNER on hearing that Reagan had won the
> California gubernatorial race

It's just too bad we can't have an epidemic of botulism.
> *California governor RONALD REAGAN in 1974, after reluctantly
> acceding to the demands of a terrorist group, the Symbionese
> Liberation Army, in releasing $2 million worth of surplus food to
> poor Californians. Reagan later wrote to a congressman that his
> comment "was one of those exaggerations that we all at times utter to
> express frustration, and we do so with the confidence that no one
> takes us literally."*

Thanks very much for sending me the clipping. . . . I have never felt
so young and virile.
> *California governor RONALD REAGAN, responding to a friend who
> sent a clipping in which a state senator charged that, "Illegitimate
> births to teenage mothers have increased alarmingly while Reagan has
> been in office."*

The thought of being President frightens me and I do not think I want the job.

RONALD REAGAN *in 1973*

Anyone . . . can be elected governor. I'm proof of that.

Georgia governor JOE FRANK HARRIS *in 1989, on his possible successor*

These are human beings. This disturbs me. I don't know why.

New York governor MARIO CUOMO *in 1990, saying he will probably sign into law a bill banning the tossing or bowling of dwarfs*

How's that shit-house of an Eastern Shore?

Maryland governor WILLIAM DONALD SCHAEFER *greets a group of legislators with a pejorative description of a district in his state*

Thirty years ago, I would have tried.

Georgia House speaker TOM MURPHY *to fellow representative Anne Mueller after she protested having her microphone switched off, saying, "Mr. Speaker, will you please turn me on?"*

◆

The cure for admiring the House of Lords is to go and look at it.

WALTER BAGEHOT

If there's a plastic surgeon who claims to be responsible for this face, then New York State will decertify him immediately.

> MARIO CUOMO *in 1991, on groundless rumors that he*
> *has had plastic surgery*

You Can't Understand City Hall, Much Less Fight It

My first qualification for mayor of the city of New York is my monumental ingratitude to each and all of you.

> FIORELLO LAGUARDIA, *shouting to his supporters at his headquarters*
> *on the night of his first election victory*

I prefer to be chastised now and understood later.

> JEAN DRAPEAU, *mayor of Montreal*

Now people can come here and watch a Vikings game and stay for the weekend. It's a different world when you have a megamall.

> KURT LAUGHINGHOUSE, *mayor of Bloomington, Minnesota, on his*
> *city's planned 78-acre Mall of America*

You're talking about a place where the police commissioner, the mayor and 25 reporters know that if they went across the street they could buy marijuana and that the guy who sells it doesn't have to worry about being arrested. That would not take place in New York.

> *New York mayor* ED KOCH *in 1988, during a visit to Amsterdam,*
> *commenting on the city's tolerance of marijuana and hashish sales*

Graffiti on the walls of trains or subway stations create bad karma.

> ED KOCH *on his antigraffiti campaign in 1989*

If you feel guilty, see a priest.

> ED KOCH *in 1988, launching his campaign to discourage people from giving money to panhandlers and homeless people on the city's subways*

I want to come back as me.

> ED KOCH *in 1988, on the subject of reincarnation*

---◆---

> *It is difficult for men in high office to avoid the malady of self-delusion. They are always surrounded by worshippers. They are constantly, and for the most part sincerely, assured of their greatness.*
>
> CALVIN COOLIDGE

There's nothing in Oakland I want.

> ART AGNOS, *mayor of San Francisco, in 1989. Agnos declined to make the traditional bet with World Series rival mayor Lionel Wilson of Oakland.*

Outside of the killings, we have one of the lowest crime rates in the country.

> MARION BARRY, *mayor of Washington, D.C., in 1989*

I am Eduardo!
> ED KOCH *in 1989, shortly before being booed off the stage at a Latin American music concert*

I say this a lot, and I probably shouldn't: the difference between rape and seduction is salesmanship.
> BILL CARPENTER, *mayor of Independence, Missouri, in 1990*

I'm pro-death. I believe in the death penalty. Let's get on with it.
> *Chicago mayor* RICHARD M. DALEY *in 1990*

I'm going to call and see how many people they're bringing. This could be a big boon to our restaurants.

> JIM NAUGLE, *mayor of Fort Lauderdale, Florida, in 1991, on hearing that the National Association to Advance Fat Acceptance was planning a convention in his city*

I think we're on the road to coming up with answers that I don't think any of us in total feel we have the answers to.

> KIM ANDERSON, *mayor of Naples, Florida, in 1991, on the community's management troubles*

The Education Presidents

Hearing some of what you've done made me ashamed of the time that I cheated in English literature on Shakespeare.

> *President* RONALD REAGAN *in 1983, at a White House ceremony honoring an adult literacy group*

We think there is a parallel between federal involvement in education and the decline in profit over recent years.

> RONALD REAGAN *in 1983, explaining his misgivings about undue emphasis on government spending on education*

Because he uses too big a words.

> RONALD REAGAN *in 1986, explaining why he seldom quotes William F. Buckley, Jr.*

Well, I guess that's enough of a history lesson here for today.

> RONALD REAGAN *in 1987, after describing to a group of high school*
> *students how his dog Rex won't go into Lincoln's bedroom,*
> *encouraging Reagan to believe that Lincoln's ghost is there*

Facts are stupid things.

> RONALD REAGAN *addressing the Republican National Convention*
> *in 1988. He was misquoting John Adams, who in 1770*
> *wrote, "Facts are stubborn things; and whatever may be our*
> *wishes, our inclinations, or the dictates of our passions, they*
> *cannot alter the state of facts and evidence."*

◆

Practical politics consists in ignoring facts.

> HENRY BROOKS ADAMS

Pushed the button down here and one up here with the green thing
on it. And out came a command to somebody that I had written.

> President GEORGE BUSH *marveling over the capabilities of a personal*
> *computer newly installed in the Oval Office, and which he had just*
> *been trained to use*

These questions. . . . Something's going awry here. I mean, if I just
listen to the question, I can answer whatever it is. But if I think it's

going to be on [the script], I don't listen to the question, I just look at [the script].

> GEORGE BUSH *in 1991, inadvertently speaking into an open microphone, complaining that questions during a "spontaneous" question-and-answer session with a teachers' group were not going in the order his staff had prepared him for*

---◆---

I know how to read a Tele-Prompter! I can run the country now!

> Writer-turned-broadcaster MICHAEL KINSLEY, on becoming co-anchor of CNN's "Crossfire" program, in 1990

And let me say in conclusion, thanks for the kids. I learned an awful lot about bathtub toys—about how to work the telephone. One guy knows—several of them know their own telephone numbers—preparation to go to the dentist. A lot of things I'd forgotten. So it's been a good day.

> GEORGE BUSH *in 1992, at a Head Start center in Catonsville, Maryland*

The Feminist Presidents

The greatest thing for any woman is to be a wife and mother.

THEODORE ROOSEVELT

Sensible and responsible women do not want to vote.

GROVER CLEVELAND *in 1905*

If it wasn't for women, us men would still be walking around in skin suits carrying clubs.

President RONALD REAGAN *in 1983, addressing a convention of women's organizations*

Hey, listen, I'm a member of the NRA. You're hurting my feelings, as they say in China.

GEORGE BUSH *in 1989, asked why he didn't condemn violence against women when speaking before an audience of what he labels the "macho" National Rifle Association*

◆

In our family, I'm the boss.

Russian president BORIS YELTSIN in 1992, during a visit to the United States, when asked during a television interview about the influence exerted on him by his wife Naina

---

The Vice Presidents

Anyone who thinks that the Vice President can take a position independent of the President of his administration simply has no knowledge of politics or government. You are his choice in a political marriage, and he expects your absolute loyalty.

> *Former vice president* HUBERT HUMPHREY *in 1969, ridiculing suggestions that Vice President Spiro Agnew was acting without President Richard Nixon's endorsement in lashing out at the "parasites of passion" and "ideological eunuchs" in the press who dared criticize the Nixon administration*

---- ◆ ----

> *My country has in its wisdom contrived for me the most insignificant office that ever the invention of man contrived or his imagination conceived.*
>
> JOHN ADAMS on the vice presidency, in 1793

There's no difference between me and the president on taxes. No more nit-picking. Zip-a-dee-doo-dah. Now it's off to the races.

> GEORGE BUSH *in the mid-1980s on his working relationship with President Reagan*

My position is like Ronald Reagan's. Put that down, mark it down. Good, you got it.

> GEORGE BUSH *in the mid-1980s on working with Reagan*

I'm for Mr. Reagan—blindly.

> GEORGE BUSH *on working with Reagan*

I haven't sat down and talked with George Bush on this, so I can't go in and tell you anything.

> DAN QUAYLE *in 1988, asked for details on his campaign promise that a Bush administration would ensure that anyone wanting a college education would get one*

---◆---

The second office of the government is honorable and easy, the first is but a splendid misery.

> THOMAS JEFFERSON on the vice presidency and the presidency, respectively, in 1797

The Historical Revisionists

Quebec has been disadvantaged in the auto industry since Confederation.

> *Quebec industry minister* RODRIQUE TREMBLAY *in 1979. The act of Confederation that created Canada took place in 1867.*

The Sandinistas came in. They overthrew Somoza, killed him and overthrew him. Killed him, threw him out.

> GEORGE BUSH *in 1984, displaying faulty knowledge of the plight of Somoza, who escaped Nicaragua during a coup to overthrow him and was later assassinated in Paraguay*

England was always very proud of the fact that the English police did not have to carry guns. . . . In England, if a criminal carried a gun, even though he didn't use it, he was not tried for burglary or theft or whatever he was doing. He was tried for first-degree murder and hung if he was found guilty.

> *President* RONALD REAGAN *in 1982, on British legal traditions. Informed that the story is "just not true," White House spokesman Larry Speakes said, "Well, it's a good story, though. It made the point, didn't it?"*

They just want to kill. They have a spirit of murder. Abortionists are worse than [deposed Romanian leader Nicolai] Ceausescu, worse than Stalin.

> *Evangelist and former presidential candidate* PAT ROBERTSON *in 1990, on pro-choice politicians*

Bad Science

The brute theory has paralyzed the influence of many of our preachers and undermined the faith of many of our young people in college.

> *Perennial presidential candidate* WILLIAM JENNINGS BRYAN *in 1923, shedding his credibility with his observations on "the brute theory" (evolution)*

I think the fact that children have been prematurely born even down to the three-month stage and have lived to, the record shows, to grow up and be normal human beings, that ought to be enough for all of us.

> RONALD REAGAN, *speaking in 1982 to a group of religion editors. At the end of three months, a fetus is 3 1/2 inches long; there is no record of a three-month fetus surviving premature birth.*

I've not tied my life by it, but I won't answer the question the other way because I don't know enough about it to say, is there something to it or not.

> RONALD REAGAN *in 1988, when asked if he believed in astrology. Asked about the Astrology President, House speaker Jim Wright said, "I'm glad he consults somebody."*

◆

The typical lawmaker of today is a man wholly devoid of principle—a mere counter in a grotesque and knavish game. If the right pressure could be applied to him he would be cheerfully in favor of polygamy, astrology or cannibalism.

> H. L. MENCKEN in 1930

Eco-Awareness

A tree is a tree. How many more do you need to look at?

> *California governor* RONALD REAGAN *in 1966, opposing expansion of California's Redwoods Park*

The American Petroleum Institute filed suit against the Environmental Protection Agency [and] charged that the agency was suppressing a scientific study for fear it might be misinterpreted. . . . The suppressed study reveals that 80 percent of air pollution comes not from chimneys and auto exhaust pipes, but from plants and trees.

Presidential candidate RONALD REAGAN, *in 1979. There is no scientific data to support Reagan's assertion.*

---◆---

If you don't say anything, you won't be called on to repeat it.
CALVIN COOLIDGE

I know Teddy Kennedy had fun at the Democratic convention when he said that I had said that trees and vegetation cause 80 percent of the air pollution in this country. Well, now he was a little wrong about what I said. First of all, I didn't say air pollution. I said oxides of nitrogen. And I'm right. Growing and decaying vegetation in this land are responsible for 93 percent of the oxides of nitrogen.

Presidential candidate RONALD REAGAN *in 1980. Reagan was confusing nitrous oxide, which vegetation does emit, with nitrogen dioxide, which smokestacks emit. Kennedy had quoted Reagan accurately.*

I have flown twice over Mount St. Helens out on our West Coast. I'm not a scientist and I don't know the figures, but I have a suspicion that that one little mountain has probably released more sulphur dioxide into the atmosphere of the world than has been released in the last ten years of automobile driving or things of that kind that people are so concerned about.

> *Presidential candidate* RONALD REAGAN *in 1980. At its peak activity, the volcanic Mount St. Helens emitted about 2,000 tons of sulphur dioxide per day, compared with 81,000 tons of the pollutant emitted each day by cars.*

Trees cause more pollution than automobiles.

> RONALD REAGAN *in 1981*

If environmentalists had their way, we'd all be living in rabbits' holes and birds' nests.

> RONALD REAGAN *in 1981*

Maybe we can get Mrs. Reagan to wear a coyote coat.

> JAMES WATT, *interior secretary in the Reagan administration, in 1982, on his opinion that coyotes should be killed off*

A left-wing cult dedicated to bringing down the type of government I believe in.

> JAMES WATT *in 1982, describing the environmental movement*

Look what happened to Germany in the 1930s. The dignity of man was subordinated to the powers of Nazism. . . . Those are the forces that this can evolve into.

> JAMES WATT *in 1983, equating environmentalists with Nazis*

You've got that whole expanse of ocean. It isn't as if you were looking at the ocean through a little frame, and now somebody put something in the way. . . . We've got a lot of freighters . . . up in mothballs. Why don't we bring down some and anchor them between the shore and the oil derrick? And then the people would see a ship, and they wouldn't find anything wrong with that at all.

> *President* RONALD REAGAN *in 1985, defending offshore drilling*
> *to a reporter in Santa Barbara, California, and offering an*
> *aesthetic solution*

I don't think they'll be happy until the White House looks like a bird's nest.

> RONALD REAGAN *in 1983, coming to the defense of his embattled*
> *Environmental Protection Agency chief Anne Burford, whose*
> *resignation he had just accepted—an event brought on, Reagan said,*
> *by Burford critics who acted out of "environmental extremism"*

There is today in the United States as much forest as there was when Washington was at Valley Forge.

> RONALD REAGAN *in 1983, speaking to lumbermen in Oregon*

Caribou like the pipeline. They lean up against it, have a lot of babies, scratch on it. There's more damn caribou than you can shake a stick at.

> GEORGE BUSH *in 1987, dismissing claims by environmentalists who*
> *fear the Alaska pipeline will reduce the caribou population*

Nobody's told me the difference between a red squirrel, a black one or a brown one. . . . Do we have to save every subspecies?

MANUEL LUJAN, *George Bush's interior secretary with responsibility for enforcing the Endangered Species Act, responding to concerns that the red squirrel was threatened by the construction of an observatory*

Anyone who sees George Bush as the "environment president" at the Grand Canyon ought to look closely for Elvis, alive and well, rafting by on the Colorado River.

Senator ALBERT GORE *after Bush visited the canyon to describe his administration's antipollution efforts in 1991*

I know they are all environmentalists. I heard a lot of my speeches recycled.

JESSE JACKSON *referring in 1991 to the men seeking the Democratic presidential nomination*

I beat the reds, and now I'm going to beat the greens.

MAGNUS MALAN, *demoted from South African defense minister to the forestry portfolio, vows to apply his anti-Communist zeal to meddlesome environmentalists, in 1991*

The left doesn't have a monopoly on ecology. We at the National Front respect life and love animals. I myself have a white rat whom I kiss every day on the mouth.

French ultraconservative politician JEAN-MARIE LE PEN *in 1991*

◆

In politics, nothing is contemptible.

BENJAMIN DISRAELI

We want to save the little furry-feathery guy and all of that, but I don't want to see 40,000 loggers thrown out of work.

> GEORGE BUSH *campaigning in New Hampshire in 1992, on the endangered status of the soon-to-expire Endangered Species Act, which protects animals such as the scarce northern spotted owl of the Pacific Northwest*

It was so hard on the daffodils.

> MARGARET THATCHER *in April 1992, after an angry woman struck her on the head with a bunch of flowers*

How's That Again?

Do not compute the totality of your poultry population until all the manifestations of incubation have been entirely completed.

> WILLIAM JENNINGS BRYAN, *on the appropriate moment to begin counting one's chickens*

You cannot roast a wet blanket.

> *Canadian prime minister* MACKENZIE KING *in parliamentary debate*

Q: What shall we do about the Abortion Bill?
A: Pay it!

> *Attributed to* PIERRE TRUDEAU, *speaking to an aide*

It would be like sticking my head in a moose.

> *Toronto mayor* ALLAN LAMPORT, *describing what it would be like to vote for a proposed measure*

You can lead a dead horse to water, but you can't make him drink.

> *Toronto mayor* ALLAN LAMPORT

If this thing starts to snowball it will catch fire right across the country.

> ROBERT THOMPSON, *former Social Credit leader in Canada*

Here comes the orator, with his flood of words and his drop of reason.

BENJAMIN FRANKLIN in 1735

Now the only thing that remains unresolved is the resolution of the problem.

> *Ontario education minister* TOM WELLS *in 1976*

Mr. Speaker, there are two visitors in the House today. Miss Conny Lingus from Cherryvale and Mr. Jack Meoff from Falkland. Please make them feel welcome.

> PATRICIA JORDAN, *a British Columbia legislator, unwittingly introduces to members of the assembly two fictitious individuals, whose names were slipped to her by mischievous reporters from the legislative press gallery on April Fool's Day 1976*

The specificity of the totality.

> JOE CLARK, *leader of Canada's Progressive Conservative Party, in 1983*

Reagan Ronald.

> *Signature written in haste by* RONALD REAGAN *on a tax-reform bill in 1986*

Win just one for the Gippet.

> RONALD REAGAN, *blowing his most famous movie-career line about the Gipper at the 1988 Notre Dame dedication of the Knute Rockne postage stamp*

--- ◆ ---

You really don't want a President who is a football fan. Football combines the worst features of American life. It is violence punctuated by committee meetings.

> Columnist GEORGE WILL in his 1990 book, *Men at Work: The Craft of Baseball*

There are various groups that think you can ban certain kinds of—certain kinds of guns. And I am not in that mode. I am in the mode of being deeply concerned.

> GEORGE BUSH *in 1989, offering a deeply confusing response to calls for a ban on assault rifles*

Even though there may be some misguided critics of what we're trying to do, I think they're on the wrong path.

> RONALD REAGAN *in 1987*

James Bond is a man of honor, a symbol of real value to the free world.

> RONALD REAGAN *in 1983, in a television tribute to the fictional spy*

If you could add together the power of prayer of the people just in this room, what would be its megatonnage?

> RONALD REAGAN *in 1984, during a White House prayer breakfast*

Bushisms

I will never apologize for the United States of America—I don't care what the facts are.

> *Vice President* GEORGE BUSH, *speaking to Republican ethnic leaders about the accidental downing of an Iranian airliner*

America is in crying need of the moral vision you have brought to our political life. . . . What great goals you have!

>GEORGE BUSH *in 1986 in conversation with evangelist Jerry Falwell*

That was a Freudian slip.

>GEORGE BUSH *in 1989, speaking to a meeting of the AFL-CIO, which he referred to as the AFL-CIA*

Oh, well, they will, er, uh. This is not a personal thing.

>GEORGE BUSH *in 1989, after a congressman told him that their telephone conversation, in which Bush had declared himself "displeased with [Congressman Richard] Gephardt," was being broadcast to reporters over a speakerphone*

Yeah, I think there's some social change going on. . . . AIDS, for example, uh, is a, is a, uh, disease for, disease of poverty in a sense. It's where the hopelessness is. It's bigger than that of course.

>GEORGE BUSH *in 1988, asked a straightforward question about why so many Americans use illicit drugs*

---◆---

When I was a boy I was told that anybody could become President; I'm beginning to believe it.

>CLARENCE DARROW

If you walk like a duck, and you quack like a duck, and say you're a duck, you're a duck.

Characteristic saying of GEORGE BUSH

It gets into quotas, go into numerical, set numbers for doctors or for, it could go into all kinds of things.

GEORGE BUSH *in 1992, trying to explain his objections to affirmative action programs*

I have opinions of my own—strong opinions—but I don't always agree with them.

GEORGE BUSH

I'm not what you call your basic intellectual.

> GEORGE BUSH, *speaking to a* New York Times *reporter in 1988. Ed Mahe, Jr., political director of the Republican National Committee when Bush was its chairman in the 1970s, said of him, "He's not a deep person."*

See that rabbit over there? Don't let him out if Millie comes to this school, okay? The other day . . . running through the woods, Millie caught something and Mrs. Bush said to the Secret Service man, "What is that?" And the Secret Service guy said, "A bunny." She had caught this bunny.

> GEORGE BUSH *in 1989, struggling for the appropriate line of small talk, tells a horrified class of 10- and 11-year-olds in Chicago about the kills achieved by the First Dog at the presidential retreat Camp David*

◆

We all recognize a steady decadence in our politics. The men in public life today are, with few exceptions, intellectually and morally inferior to the great statesmen of the war and the years which preceded it. Political preferment is less and less tempting to good men. The conditions of public life are more and more repellent. The tendency is dangerous, and it is our duty to arrest it.

> MOORFIELD STOREY, *writing in the January 1892 issue of* The Atlantic Monthly

I'm an Oyster Bay kind of guy.

GEORGE BUSH *in 1989, on how he identifies with Theodore Roosevelt*

If anyone can figure that out, call me.

GEORGE BUSH *in 1990, after seeing the film* Field of Dreams

We just want to get from you-all how it's doing down there. A lot of these guys wanna get goin', want to get on to Mars. Have you got any advice first of all for these young guys here, young kids, boys and girls?

. GEORGE BUSH *in 1992, accompanied by a group of young space cadets, in conversation with the crew of the space shuttle* Discovery

While the press is here, was there—did the Democratic governors meet, and is there any feeling that we shouldn't press to try to get something done by March 20th? Do we—is there—can anyone—is there a spokesman on that point? Because what I would like to suggest—not that you'd have to sign every 't' and 'i' but that we urge Congress to move by that date. And if that date isn't good, what date? Is there any feeling on that one?

GEORGE BUSH *in February 1992, addressing the National Governors' Association*

All I was doing was appealing for an endorsement, not suggesting you endorse it.

GEORGE BUSH *in February 1992, to Colorado Governor Roy Romer*

And in conclusion let me say this. . . . And this'll go to the Democrats who may have been smart enough to join Rotary too. There's a non-partisan—no, but I really mean this one, that from the heart in the sense that some things, at least the way I look at this.

> GEORGE BUSH *campaigning in New Hampshire in 1992*

I mean a child that doesn't have a parent to read to that child or that doesn't see that when the child is hurting to have a parent and help out or neither parent there enough to pick the kid up and dust him off and send him back into the game at school or whatever, that kid has a disadvantage.

> GEORGE BUSH *in 1992, on family life*

The Thing Man

Your dedication and tireless work with the hostage thing, with Central America, really gives me cause for great pride in you and thanks. Get some turkey, George Bush.

> GEORGE BUSH's *written note of thanks to Oliver North, circa Thanksgiving 1985, read by North on the television program "Nightline" in 1991*

[They] blame America first crowd from the post-Vietnam thing.

> GEORGE BUSH *in 1988, urging Americans to ignore those arguing against U.S. military interventionism*

Did you come here and say, "The heck with it, I don't need this darn thing?" Did you go through a withdrawal thing?

> GEORGE BUSH *in 1988, campaigning at a drug rehabilitation center in Newark, New Jersey*

The roots thing.

> GEORGE BUSH *in 1988, on plans for a film about his family vacations in Maine*

The drought thing.

> GEORGE BUSH *in 1988, on a drought crisis*

Oh, the vision thing.

> GEORGE BUSH *in 1988, when a friend suggested he go to Camp David to figure out what he should tell the voters he stands for in the upcoming presidential election*

Just put in some of that vision thing.

> GEORGE BUSH *in 1988, instructing a speech writer recently recruited to help with his campaign. When the speech writer asked, "Which aspect of your vision do you want to convey, Mr. Vice President?" Bush responded, "You know, that vision thing."*

I haven't selected *her.* But let me tell you, this gender thing is history. You're looking at a guy who sat down with Margaret Thatcher across the table and talked about serious issues.

> GEORGE BUSH *in 1988, asked about who he would select as his running mate*

But look, how was the actual deployment thing?
> GEORGE BUSH *in 1989, asking space-shuttle astronauts about the launch of the Magellan space probe*

I'm taking drops now, one in the morning and one at night, but the vision thing is very good.
> GEORGE BUSH *in 1990, on treatment for glaucoma in his left eye*

The stomach thing.
> GEORGE BUSH *in January 1992, referring to the stomach flu that marred his trip to Japan*

Vanities

I think I have a right to resent, to object to libelous statements about my dog.
> FRANKLIN ROOSEVELT *in 1944, on charges that his Scottie, Fala, had been stranded in the Aleutian Islands and was retrieved at a cost of millions of dollars to the government*

Yes, I got applause 80 times.
> *President* LYNDON JOHNSON *in 1964, on being congratulated after an address to a congressional joint session. The senator who offered the compliment checked the record and was astonished to find that LBJ was exactly right: he had been counting as he spoke.*

Now, like I'm President.
> GEORGE BUSH *in 1989, explaining to school children why it would be*
> *difficult for "some drug guy" to offer to get him high*

I am extraordinarily patient, provided I get my own way in the end.
> MARGARET THATCHER

· 3 ·

Economics

When many people are out of work, unemployment results.

CALVIN COOLIDGE

Many people have left their jobs for the more profitable one of selling apples.

> HERBERT HOOVER, *on hearing that the International Apple Shippers Association, finding itself with a surplus, had decided to sell them on credit to jobless men who resold them on street corners for 5¢ each*

A recession is a period in which you tighten your belt. In a depression, you have no belt to tighten. In a panic, you have no pants left to hold up.

> *Canadian socialist leader* T. C. (TOMMY) DOUGLAS

It's a recession when your neighbor loses his job. It's a depression when you lose yours.

HARRY TRUMAN

I walk into a store and approach a department, say the cosmetic department, and ask for a package of razor blades. I lay out a $5 bill and I will buy anything up to that amount that the salesperson suggests. Believe it or not, in trying this over ten years, I have had only two salespeople get the entire $5. American business has just forgotten the importance of selling.

Senator BARRY GOLDWATER *in 1962*

A billion here, a billion there and pretty soon you're talking about real money.

Senator EVERETT DIRKSEN *on fiscal policy*

Kings and ministers are . . . themselves always, and without any exceptions, the greatest spendthrifts in the society.

ADAM SMITH

When you spend money abroad it is not inflationary.

Canadian prime minister PIERRE TRUDEAU *in 1968, returning from a Mediterranean cruise*

Q: What does Pierre Trudeau really think about the problems of the Canadian economy when he's lying in bed at night.

A: When I'm lying in bed at night, I really don't think about the problems of the Canadian economy.

> PIERRE TRUDEAU, *responding to a student's question in a televised interview*

Let each of us ask, not just what will government do for me, but what I can do for myself.

> RICHARD NIXON *in his second inaugural address, in 1973—a line that rebuked John F. Kennedy's famous comment in his inaugural 12 years earlier: "Ask not what your country can do for you; ask what you can do for your country."*

Greed is what makes the world tick, baby.

> *Former Canadian finance minister* JOHN TURNER, *in a private twist on his public comment that, "I doubt we can change men's motives, including the drive for material benefit."*

Fascism was really the basis of the New Deal.

> RONALD REAGAN *in 1976*

Unemployment insurance is a paid vacation for freeloaders.

> RONALD REAGAN *in the late 1970s*

Voodoo economics.

> GEORGE BUSH *campaigning for the GOP presidential nomination in 1980, ridiculing the supply-side economic theories promoted by rival Ronald Reagan. Bush, after becoming Reagan's running mate, denied having made the statement, which promptly turned up on a videotape after he had challenged "anybody to find it."*

None of us really understands what's going on with all these numbers.

> *Confession by Reagan's budget director,* DAVID STOCKMAN, *in a 1981* Atlantic Monthly *article, in which he says Reagan's campaign plank of "supply-side economics . . . was always a Trojan horse to bring down the top [income tax] rate," and says of Reagan's tax-reform bill, "Do you realize the greed that came to the forefront? The hogs were really feeding." After the article appeared, Stockman was invited to lunch at the White House, and said afterward: "My visit to the Oval Office for lunch with the President was more in the nature of a visit to the woodshed after supper. . . . He was not happy about the way this has developed—and properly so." A 1982 report by the Congressional Budget Office showed that taxpayers with less than $10,000 in earnings lost an average of $240 as a result of Reagan's tax bill of the previous year, while those with more than $80,000 in earnings benefited by average gains of $15,130.*

It is possible to get to heaven in a Cadillac, but it is hard.

> *New York governor* MARIO CUOMO, *justifying a fiscal policy aimed at addressing the disparity between rich and poor*

We've got a $120 billion deficit coming, and the President says, "You know, a young man went into a grocery store and he had an orange in one hand and a bottle of vodka in the other, and he paid for the orange with food stamps and he took the change and paid for the vodka. That's what's wrong." And we just shake our heads.

> *Republican senator* ROBERT PACKWOOD *of Oregon in 1982,*
> *expressing frustration with Ronald Reagan's frequent use of obviously*
> *fictitious anecdotes that, apparently, the President, at least, believes*
> *even if no one else does. A few days after Packwood's comment,*
> *agriculture department official Mary Jarratt told Congress that the*
> *department hadn't been able to prove food-stamp abuse, and said the*
> *change from a food stamp purchase is limited to 99¢. "It's not*
> *possible to buy a bottle of vodka with 99¢."*

If the price of conventional [oil] is X, you have a price of X plus Y for the nonconventional oil, and the international price—you know what that is—but we have indicated we will continue to subsidize the prices . . . so that what you would end up with would be a mix of these prices.

> MARC LALONDE, *Canadian energy minister, explaining his*
> *government's energy policy to parliament in 1982*

No matter how we define the term, Canada has an acute shortage of rich people.

> *Canadian finance minister* MICHAEL WILSON *in 1985, defending his*
> *decision not to raise taxes on the wealthy*

I feel a sense of deja voodoo.

> LAWRENCE SUMMERS, *economic adviser to presidential candidate Michael Dukakis, on the similarities between George Bush's 1988 economic platform and that of 1980 candidate Ronald Reagan*

You can't drink yourself sober, you can't spend yourself rich, and you can't pump the prime without priming the pump. You know something? I said that backwards. . . . You can't prime the pump without pumping the prime. . . .

> *President* RONALD REAGAN *in 1982*

My fellow Americans, I've talked to you on a number of occasions about economic problems and opportunities our nation faces and I am prepared to tell you, it's a hell of a mess.

> RONALD REAGAN *in 1982, quipping during a sound check prior to a radio address*

Now we are trying to get unemployment to go up, and I think we are going to succeed.

> RONALD REAGAN *during a 1982 GOP fund-raiser speech*

This is a thousand points of light, but unfortunately the batteries aren't included.

> JAMES SASSER, *chairman of the Senate budget committee, on President Bush's first budget, in 1989*

Never get all too uptight about stuff that hasn't reached Lubbock yet.
President GEORGE BUSH *in 1989, referring to criticism among political gossips in Washington that his administration was rudderless. Lubbock is a community in Texas, which Bush once represented in Congress.*

It's a very good question, very direct, and I'm not going to answer it.
GEORGE BUSH *in 1990, on what sort of deficit-reduction proposals he would present to Congress*

---------------◆---------------

What Englishman will give his mind to politics as long as he can afford to keep a motor car?
GEORGE BERNARD SHAW, *in* The Apple Cart, *1930*

I think I've got to do better in making clear what the message is, and I think I can do better. But I think there's so much noise out there that I've got to figure out how to make it clearer that we are for the things that I have advocated that would help.
GEORGE BUSH *in 1991, on the direction he intends to steer the economy*

You can lead the House to order, but you can't make it think.
WILLIAM WELD, *governor of Massachusetts, in 1991, on his budget impasse with the state legislature*

Tripling the national debt. A $500-billion S&L crisis. Tax breaks for the wealthy with 40 million Americans in poverty. My only question is: where was Kitty Kelley when we needed her?

> WILLIAM GRAY, *House majority whip and a Democrat, on the
> economic aftermath of the Reagan years, in 1991*

◆

---

*What's in it [government] for us? Sure, if we own an aerospace
contracting company, a five-thousand-acre sugar-beet farm or
a savings and loan with the president's son on the board of
directors, we can soak Uncle Sucker for millions. But most of
us failed to plan ahead and buy McDonnell Douglas, and now
the only thing we can get out of government is government
benefits—measly VA checks and Medicare. We won't get far
on the French Riviera on this kind of chump change.*

> P. J. O'ROURKE *in* Parliament of Whores, *1991*

Things change. The tide comes in, it comes out. The moon goes up, it comes down.

> NICHOLAS BRADY, *George Bush's treasury secretary, responds to an
> interviewer's question about what measures might bring the United
> States out of recession*

You can slice me up, but that won't last you for long.

> *Russian president* BORIS YELTSIN *in 1992, to a woman who asked
> him what the people could eat during a time of food shortages*

A government is not an old pair of socks that you throw out. Come to think of it, you don't throw out old pairs of socks anyway these days.

> *Russian president* BORIS YELTSIN *in 1992,*
> *during a period of shortage*
> *of food and basic goods*

I haven't really been able to sort out exactly why there has been this degree of pessimism.

> GEORGE BUSH *in December 1991, during the*
> *18th month of the longest, if not the deepest*
> *recession since the Depression*

Could be. Or might do something radical like reduce the deficit, which seems to me—some people have a great interest in, including me.

> GEORGE BUSH *in 1992, asked if a reduction in military spending might make possible more spending on domestic programs*

In politics the choice is always between two evils.
> JOHN MORELY, British statesman

[The year] ended with the concern for Americans that are hurting because of this sluggish economy. I mean, when families are having trouble making ends meet or are thinking even if they have a job, I might not have one tomorrow. Fear. You worry about that. I worry a lot about that.

> GEORGE BUSH *in 1992*

We're enjoying sluggish times, and not enjoying them very much.
> GEORGE BUSH *in 1992*

If a frog had wings, he wouldn't hit his tail on the ground. "If." Too hypothetical.

> GEORGE BUSH *in 1992, on the inadvisability of extending unemployment benefits*

I've watched the eyes of a gruff, gray-haired businessman grow wet as he spoke of having to lay off people who'd kept his small shop running for years. I've seen worry in the face of a farm worker idled by a killer arctic freeze. . . . And I've seen the kindly face of a carpenter who could find no work framing houses and now makes children's toys for free.

> *California governor* PETE WILSON *in 1992. Reporters, unable to track down any of Wilson's victims of hardship, were told by the governor's office that they were "a composite."*

Taxing Matters

The promises of yesterday are the taxes of today.
> *Canadian prime minister* MACKENZIE KING *in 1931*

♦

There is no art which one government sooner learns of another than that of draining money from the pockets of the people.
> ADAM SMITH, on taxation

I'm anxious to have taxes reduced.

DWIGHT EISENHOWER

[I'm] committed to tax reform.

RICHARD NIXON

I stand for lower taxes.

GERALD FORD

I believe we can cut taxes.

JIMMY CARTER

I will not raise taxes.

RONALD REAGAN

There can be no moral justification for the progressive income tax.

RONALD REAGAN, *in a syndicated radio broadcast, in 1978*

Who better to talk a tax increase to death than Jack Kemp?

Congressman JACK KEMP *in 1989*

I want to hold the line on taxes.

GEORGE BUSH

Read my lips, no new taxes.

GEORGE BUSH, *campaigning in 1988*

◆

It is dangerous for a national candidate to say things people might remember.

EUGENE MCCARTHY

Read my hips.

> GEORGE BUSH *in 1990, ducking reporters who asked him*
> *how he intended to break a budget impasse with Congress*
> *without resorting to a tax hike. The President was jogging at the*
> *time. In June 1990, the White House issued a statement saying*
> *"tax revenue increases" were imminent, thus breaking the 1988*
> *promise of no new taxes, but Bush was careful not to let the*
> *expression drop from his lips.*

Seers in High Places

No Congress of the United States ever assembled, on surveying the state of the Union, has met with a more pleasing prospect than that which appears at the present time.

> CALVIN COOLIDGE *in December 1928*

Conditions are fundamentally sound.

> HERBERT HOOVER'*s description of the economy in December 1929*

The Depression is over.

> HERBERT HOOVER *in June 1930. Hoover chose*
> *the word "depression" because it seemed less apocalyptic than*
> *"panic," the term commonly used until the thirties to*
> *describe sharp*
> *economic downturns.*

◆

Since a politician never believes what he says, he is surprised to be taken at his word.

CHARLES DE GAULLE in 1962

The recession will be mild and the whole country will come out of it in not too many months from now.

GEORGE BUSH *in January 1991, as the economy moved into the most painful phase of its downturn*

I probably have made mistakes in assessing the fact that the economy would recover. I think I've known, look, this economy is in a free-fall.

GEORGE BUSH *in January 1992, as the stock market, setting record highs, was signaling the beginnings of an economic upturn*

· 4 ·

Race Relations

Segregation of the races is proper and the only practical and correct way of life in our states.

> *Florida judge* HARROLD CARSWELL *in 1948. This comment from a Carswell speech, dug up by a reporter years later, caused the Senate to reject Richard Nixon's attempt to appoint Carswell to the Supreme Court in 1969.*

Can they reach Oxford, Mississippi?

> *Attorney General* ROBERT KENNEDY *in 1962, wondering if Soviet missiles recently discovered in Cuba could be of any use against segregationalist rioters attempting to prevent James Meredith from becoming the first African American to be enrolled at "Ole Miss," the State University of Mississippi at Oxford*

I draw the line in the dust and toss the gauntlet before the feet of tyranny. And I say—segregation now, segregation tomorrow, segregation forever.

GEORGE WALLACE *in 1963, in his inaugural address as governor of Alabama*

The only reason we need ZIP codes is because niggers can't read.

Virginia senator WILLIAM SCOTT, *who declined to run for reelection in 1978. On another occasion, Pentagon officials attempting to brief Scott on missile silos were interrupted by Scott, who said, "Wait a minute, I'm not interested in agriculture. I want the military stuff."*

Some of them have marvellous minds, those black people over there.

CHARLES Z. WICK, *Ronald Reagan's director of the U.S. Information Agency, in 1983*

You people married Italian men, you know what it's like.

Vice-presidential candidate GERALDINE FERRARO *in 1984, explaining that she wants to release details of her financial status but has not yet been able to convince husband John Zaccaro to cooperate*

You know, back home, Bubba still thinks we ought to just speak English in this country.

Democratic governor WALLACE WILKINSON *of Kentucky in 1988, on how his constituents might react to Michael Dukakis's bilingualism*

                                     ◆

A democracy is a government in the hands of men of low birth, no property, and vulgar employments.

ARISTOTLE

Republicans many times can't get the words "equality of opportunity" out of their mouths. Their lips do not form that way.

> *Republican Congressman* JACK KEMP *in 1988, urging his party to try harder to appeal to minority voters*

A militant.

> GEORGE BUSH, *speaking of Dr. Martin Luther King, Jr.*

The little brown ones.

> *Presidential candidate* GEORGE BUSH *in 1988, pointing out three of his grandchildren, who are Mexican Americans, to President Reagan. Defending his comment the next day, Bush said, "For anyone to suggest that that comment of pride is anything other than what it was, I find personally offensive."*

We used to have minstrel shows when I was in grade school. Of course, today you can't do that, everybody blackfaced up. . . . I think it's too bad.

> *House minority leader* ROBERT MICHEL *in 1988. Michel later apologized for the comment on* "USA Today: The Television Show."

It's all sorts of middle-aged white men in suits—forests of middle-aged men in dark suits. All slightly red-faced from eating and drinking too much.

DIANE ABBOTT, *the only black member of the British parliament, on her colleagues, in 1988*

Black preachers start out not intending to make sense. They create a kind of psychological connection. You end up crying. You end up feeling good. You end up thinking about your mama, and you go away fulfilled. But you're not a bit better off.

Atlanta mayor ANDREW YOUNG, *joking about his fellow African-American preachers in 1988*

To be quite frank, I could care less.

Civil rights hero JAMES MEREDITH *in 1989, when asked if it bothers him that his boss, Senator Jesse Helms, has opposed most civil rights legislation*

I don't live on Pete Stark's plantation.

LOUIS SULLIVAN, *federal secretary of health and human services, who is black, to a 1990 claim by California congressman Stark, who is white, that Sullivan is "a disgrace to his race" for supporting Republican social policies*

You know Gus Hawkins, that little black man from California? Well, he's 100 percent black, you know, but he looks white.

Ohio congressman BUZ LUKENS *on fellow congressman Augustus Hawkins of California, in 1990*

There are different Klans—just like there's different fraternities at a college.

> *Louisiana state representative* DAVID DUKE *in 1990, explaining his former Klan leadership*

I'm not against the blacks, and a lot of the good blacks will attest to that.

> *Former Arizona governor* EVAN MECHAM *in 1990, on being called antiblack*

Toms come in all sizes and ages. There are uneducated Toms and educated Toms.

> *Illinois congressman* GUS SAVAGE, *who is black, in 1990, on his Oxford-educated congressional opponent, who is also black*

---◆---

> *Government remains the paramount field of unwisdom because it is there that men seek power over others—and lose it over themselves.*
>
> BARBARA TUCHMAN in 1980

Is that racist?

> D. A. COON, *mayor of Petersburg, Alaska, after telling a joke about "barbecued black boys" in 1991*

I've called it Martin Luther Coon Day all along and I think I have a right to do that because my last name is Coon. How does that grab you?

> *Mayor D. A.* COON *on why he objects to Martin Luther King, Jr. Day as an official holiday*

Slaves.

> *Montana senator* CONRAD BURNS, *telling civil rights lobbyists what was being auctioned off at a mock "slave auction" conducted by his son's confirmation class. The lobbyists were shocked, given that*

*Burns's invitation to them to attend the event came minutes after the
1991 passage of a civil rights bill in Congress.*

Why are we more shocked when a dozen people are killed in Vilnius
than [by] a massacre in Burundi? Because they are white people.
That's who we are. That's where America comes from.

Presidential candidate PATRICK BUCHANAN *in a 1991 interview with
Britain's* Sunday Telegraph. *Buchanan, who once described Adolph
Hitler as "an individual of great courage . . . extraordinary gifts,"
began his run for the presidency by worrying that Judeo-Christian
values in America were in danger of being dumped into "some landfill
called multiculturalism."*

The first black president will be a politician who is black.

Governor DOUG WILDER *of Virginia in 1992, on the presidency,
which he briefly sought in 1991–92*

·5·

War and Peace

War involves in its purposes such a train of unforeseen and unsupposed circumstances that no human wisdom can calculate the end. It has but one thing certain, and that is to increase taxes.

THOMAS PAINE *in 1787*

If [General] McClellan is not using the army, I should like to borrow it for a while.

ABRAHAM LINCOLN *in 1862, on McClellan's reluctance to take on the Confederate forces*

My home policy: I wage war; my foreign policy: I wage war. All the time I wage war.

GEORGES CLEMENCEAU, *in a speech to the French Chamber of Deputies in March 1918*

And while I am talking to you mothers and fathers, I give you one more assurance. I have said this before, but I shall say it again and again and again: Your boys are not going to be sent into any foreign wars.

> FRANKLIN ROOSEVELT *campaigning for reelection in 1940*

––––––––––––––––––––– ♦ –––––––––––––––––––––

The object of oratory is not truth but persuasion.

> THOMAS MACAULAY

Conscription if necessary, but not necessarily conscription.

> MACKENZIE KING, *wartime prime minister of Canada, addressing Parliament in 1942*

You always have to remember when you're dealing with generals and admirals, most of them, they're wrong a good deal of the time. Even Washington knew that; he kept warning the people, and Jefferson too, warning the people against letting the generals give you too much advice. I told you. They're most of them just like horses with blinders on. They can't see beyond the ends of their noses, most of them.

> HARRY TRUMAN, *recalling that when he became president in 1945 he was told the war in Europe would last another six months, and the war with Japan another year and a half. Germany surrendered 25 days later, Japan four months later.*

It was involuntary. They sank my boat.

> JOHN F. KENNEDY *on how he became a war hero. His patrol boat was*
> *rammed by a Japanese warship.*

You always assume that the military and intelligence people have some secret skill not available to ordinary mortals.

> JOHN F. KENNEDY *contemplating a CIA plan to back anti-Castro*
> *forces in an uprising against the new Communist regime in Cuba by*
> *means of an invasion at the Bay of Pigs in 1961. After the fiasco,*
> *Kennedy said: "All my life I've known better than to depend on the*
> *experts. How could I have been so stupid, to let them go ahead?"*

Politics is war without bloodshed, while war is politics with bloodshed.

> MAO TSE-TUNG, *Quotations from Chairman Mao*

Lobbing one into the men's room at the Kremlin.

> *Presidential candidate* BARRY GOLDWATER *in 1964, in one*
> *of his frequent references during an abysmally unsuccessful*
> *campaign against Lyndon Johnson to the validity, under*
> *certain circumstances, of nuking an enemy power. "Push the*
> *button" was one of his favorite expressions during the*
> *campaign, whose slogan was, "In Your Heart You Know*
> *He's Right." The LBJ forces, armed with Goldwater's*
> *hawkish views about unleashing an "atomic holocaust"*
> *if the occasion warranted, quickly tagged him with the slogan,*
> *"In Your Heart You Know He Might."*

If you have a mother-in-law with only one eye and she has it in the center of her forehead, you don't keep her in the living room.

> LYNDON JOHNSON, *explaining his reluctance to discuss the progress of America's military activities in Vietnam*

Yes, I know all the bad things that happened in that war. I was in uniform for four years myself.

> President RONALD REAGAN, *referring to Nazi atrocities in a 1985 interview. Reagan served in the First Motion Picture Unit of the Army Air Corps during the Second World War and was stationed in Hollywood for the duration.*

---◆---

It surely would be very nice to have an intelligent, benevolent and omniscient government, but most of the people are neither intelligent nor benevolent, nor sufficiently informed to be good rulers. And particularly a country as big as the U.S. has hardly a chance to obtain a government freed from the pest of politicians and political gambling, which is the most confounded humbug that ever existed.

> CARL JUNG in 1939

Well, he's never seen *King's Row*.

> President RONALD REAGAN *in 1985, responding to Soviet spokesman Georgi Arbatov, who said that while Reagan prepared for a summit*

with Mikhail Gorbachev by watching taped interviews, Gorbachev prepared by reading official briefing papers and probably hasn't watched any of Reagan's films because, "They are B-rated anyway." It is later reported that during the two-day summit in Geneva, Reagan said to the Soviet leader, "Do one thing for me. Tell Arbatov they weren't all B-movies."

You might be interested to know that the Scriptures are on our side on this.
RONALD REAGAN, *defending his arms-buildup program in 1985*

Well, I don't think I've ever used the Bible to further political ends or not, but I've found that the Bible contains an answer to just about everything and every problem that confronts us.
RONALD REAGAN *in 1985, after being criticized for saying the Scriptures sanction an arms buildup*

— ◆ —

Politics are not the task of a Christian.
DIETRICH BONHOEFFER, No Rusty Swords

[**L**ibya is] capable of destroying America and breaking its nose.
Libyan dictator MUAMMAR QADDAFI *in 1986*

Every time we get into the selling stage, the [costs] go down. When we get into the building stage, the costs go up.

> Senator SAM NUNN *in 1988, referring to the Pentagon's downscaling of the estimated cost of the Strategic Defense Initiative (Star Wars) from $150 billion to $69 billion*

I've often wondered, what if all of us in the world discovered that we were threatened by an outer—a power from outer space, from another planet?

> President RONALD REAGAN, *architect of the Star Wars defense policy, in 1988*

---------------◆---------------

Uneasy lies the head that wears the crown.
> WILLIAM SHAKESPEARE

This is Pearl Harbor Day. Forty-seven years ago to this very day, we were hit and hit hard at Pearl Harbor.

> GEORGE BUSH, *addressing the American Legion in Louisville, Kentucky, on September 7, 1988, three months off target*

The word is not *covert*, it's *overt*. *Covert* means you're out in the open. *Overt* is what I did. That means you're undercover.

> *Nevada senator* CHIC HECHT, *describing his career as an Army intelligence officer behind the Iron Curtain*

If that plane doesn't fly, the debate is over. It is far too expensive to be a Stealth taxi.

> *Senator* SAM NUNN *in 1989, on his Senate Armed Services Committee's decision to withhold funds for production of the B-2 bomber until the Pentagon proves it can perform as advertised*

B-2 or not B-2. That is the question.

> *Massachusetts congressman* EDWARD MARKEY *in 1989, during the debate on funding for the Stealth bomber*

To be a great president, you have to have a war. All the great presidents have had their wars.

> *U.S. Admiral* J. CROWE *in November 1990, as U.S. military preparations against Iraq were underway*

This man is a loser . . . a person who has taken hostages cruelly, brutally, a person who has hidden behind the skirts of women and children.

> *British prime minister* MARGARET THATCHER *in 1990, on Saddam Hussein. Saddam's official Iraqi News Agency responded: "The old hag Thatcher . . . would do well to remember that the empire on whose possessions the sun did not go down has long been defunct, and neither she nor any of her allies will be able to set the clock back."*

There are only two groups that are beating the drums for war in the Middle East—the Israeli Defense Ministry and its amen corner in the United States.

Columnist PATRICK BUCHANAN, *objecting to U.S. military action to drive Iraqi forces out of Kuwait in 1990*

We don't want war. We hate war. We know what war does.

Iraqi president SADDAM HUSSEIN *in 1990, about a month before invading Kuwait*

You have made clear to Saddam Hussein that he has made the greatest and most serious mistake in the desert since Warren Beatty made *Ishtar*. . . . Sorry, Mr. President—it's a Los Angeles crowd.

California gubernatorial candidate PETE WILSON *in 1990, introducing George Bush at a political event*

♦

Politics are almost as exciting as war, and quite as dangerous.
In war you can only be killed once, but in politics many times.
WINSTON CHURCHILL *in 1920*

If we get into an armed situation, he's going to get his ass kicked.
GEORGE BUSH *in 1990, to a congressional delegation in reference to*
Saddam Hussein

The great duel, the mother of all battles, has begun.
SADDAM HUSSEIN *in a radio broadcast on January 17, 1991, as*
Iraq's mother of all defeats got underway

I will remember I was in the desert.
Alabama congressman SONNY CALAHAN, *noting where he was*
when the Persian Gulf war started—at a luxury resort in Palm
Springs, California

If I could find a way to get him out of there, even putting a contract
out on him, if the CIA did that sort of thing, assuming it ever did, I
would be for it.
RICHARD NIXON *in 1991, counseling George Bush to eliminate*
Saddam Hussein with extreme prejudice

Politics is the art of looking for trouble, finding it everywhere, diagnosing it incorrectly, and applying the wrong remedies.

Groucho Marx

Those damned drums are keeping me up all night.

> GEORGE BUSH *in early 1991, complaining about the drumbeat across the street from the White House kept up by protesters against the Persian Gulf war*

If the alternative to dying is sitting out in the sun for another summer then that's not a bad alternative. . . . I'm not General Custer.

> *General* NORMAN SCHWARZKOPF *in 1991, recalling the argument he used in persuading his political bosses to allow a delay of a few weeks before attacking Iraq until he was adequately prepared to strike*

I don't know about "handed over," but "out of there" would have been nice—ex-pluperfect past tense, I mean.

> GEORGE BUSH *in 1992, responding to David Frost's question, "Do you sometimes wish that as a condition of the ceasefire you had asked for Saddam Hussein to be handed over?" William Safire, New York Times language columnist, wrote, "There is, of course, no 'ex-pluperfect past tense,'" but defended the self-described Education President as having both a precise knowledge of his tenses and a desire "to avoid the appearance of elitism"—in keeping with his habit of dropping his participial g's, for instance. (From the same interview:*

"I don't know what dramatic change that would . . . have made in terms of gettin' Saddam out of there.") The same logic, possibly, explains Bush's chronic mispronunciations of the Iraqi leader's name as "Saadam" or "Sodom."

Part of the great success was the fact we have an all volunteer army, and part of the all—the military. And part of the rationale is people will have more say in what they want to do. So a mother—I want to be a part of this. I can respect that and understand it.

GEORGE BUSH *in 1992, attempting to explain his views about the role of women in the military*

What a great saving!

Former Chilean dictator AUGUSTO PINOCHET *in 1991, reacting to news that victims of his 1973 coup had been buried two to a coffin*

·6·

Foreign Affairs

Diplomacy, American-Style

These yankee politicians are the lowest race of thieves in existence.
Canadian justice minister JOHN THOMPSON *expressing frustration after meeting with his U.S. negotiating counterparts over a dispute about fishing rights in the 1880s*

Canadians like to indulge themselves as a harmless luxury in a feeling of hostility to the United States. Practically this does not operate at all. Practically Canada will take an American, [William] Van Horne, to run its railways system and America will take a Canadian, [James] Hill, to run its. . . . But the average Canadian likes to feel patriotic by jeering at the man across the border, just as to a lesser degree the average Scotchman for similar reasons adopts a similar attitude toward England.
THEODORE ROOSEVELT, *on relations between the countries on either side of the world's longest undefended border*

The grand leap of the whale up the Fall of Niagara is esteemed, by all who have seen it, as one of the finest spectacles in nature.

> BENJAMIN FRANKLIN *in a 1765 letter to a London newspaper, poking fun at English ignorance about the American colonies*

I took the [Panama] canal zone and let Congress debate, and while the debate goes on the canal does also.

> THEODORE ROOSEVELT

He may be a son of a bitch, but he's our son of a bitch.

> FRANKLIN ROOSEVELT *on Nicaraguan dictator Anastasio Somoza*

I'll go to Japan if that's what you want. But I won't kiss their asses.

> President HARRY TRUMAN, *responding to an aide's suggestion that he visit Hiroshima for a TV program on the atomic bomb's development*

◆

Politicians neither love nor hate. Interest, not sentiment, directs them.

LORD CHESTERFIELD

I like old Joe Stalin.

HARRY TRUMAN

I was very carefully trying to avoid it because I don't know how to pronounce it. Louis St. Laurent—L-a-u-r-e-n-t. That's a French pronunciation. I wouldn't attempt to pronounce it.

> HARRY TRUMAN, *providing details of an upcoming visit to Washington by the Canadian prime minister to a reporter in 1948*

We will bury you.

> NIKITA KHRUSHCHEV's *1956 prediction of Soviet supremacy over the United States*

You'd think his caddy would have mentioned it to him.

> *Canadian external affairs minister* LESTER PEARSON *expressing his frustration after meeting with President Dwight Eisenhower over the president's ignorance about a particular Canadian concern*

I couldn't have called him an S.O.B. I didn't know he was one—at that time.

> JOHN F. KENNEDY, *responding to allegations that during a trip to Ottawa in 1961 he had scribbled on a briefing paper, "What do we do with the S.O.B. now?" For official purposes, Kennedy insisted the reference was to the Organization of American States, which the United States was urging Canada to join. Kennedy confidant Ben Bradlee later quoted Kennedy as indeed having a negative impression of Canadian prime minister John Diefenbaker: "At that time I didn't think Diefenbaker was a son of a bitch. I thought he was a prick."*

He'll do.

> JOHN F. KENNEDY *to an aide, in reference to newly elected Canadian prime minister Lester Pearson, who had just impressed Kennedy with his encyclopedic knowledge of American baseball statistics*

You pissed on my rug.

> LYNDON JOHNSON, *dressing down Lester Pearson at Camp David, Maryland, the day after Pearson called for a temporary halt in the bombing of Vietnam at a 1965 speech at Temple University in Philadelphia*

The blue-chip countries.

> RICHARD NIXON *in 1969, announcing a trip to Belgium, Britain, West Germany, Italy, and France*

That asshole.

> RICHARD NIXON's *reference to Canadian prime minister Pierre*
> *Trudeau on a tape-recorded conversation with aides in the*
> *Oval Office*

You just give me the word and I'll turn that f- - - ing island into a
parking lot.

> *Attributed to Secretary of State* ALEXANDER HAIG *by Nancy Reagan*
> *in her autobiography,* My Turn, *on advice Haig gave President*
> *Reagan about Cuba*

Um, I guess it's a yes.

> *Presidential candidate* RONALD REAGAN, *when asked if he*
> *supported continued "official relations" between the*
> *United States and Taiwan. When Beijing responded the*
> *next day with an assertion that Reagan had "insulted*
> *one billion Chinese people," he backtracked, saying,*
> *"I don't know that I said that or not, ah, I*
> *really don't . . . I mis-stated."*

[A] dispute over the sovereignty of that little ice-cold bunch of land
down there.

> RONALD REAGAN's *casual response to the decision of*
> *a loyal U.S. ally, Britain, to dispatch its armed forces to take*
> *back the Falkland Islands from invading forces of Argentina*
> *that had seized them*

Why not invite Qaddafi to San Francisco, he likes to dress up so much?

> RONALD REAGAN *in 1986, in a remark to aides reported by Bob Woodward, who wrote that Secretary of State George Shultz then added, "Why don't we give him AIDS?"*

I didn't go down there with any plan for the Americas, or anything. I went down to find out from them and [learn] their views. You'd be surprised. They're all individual countries.

> *President* RONALD REAGAN *in 1982, responding to a question about whether his Latin American trip had changed his outlook on the region*

---◆---

> *I pray Heaven to bestow the best of blessings on this house and all that shall hereafter inhabit it. May none but honest and wise men ever rule under this roof.*
>
> JOHN ADAMS in 1800, written the day after he moved into the new White House as the second president of the United States

I would say that the individuals that went there [to Spain in 1936–39 to defend the democratically elected government from the Hitler-backed forces of Francisco Franco] were, in the opinions of most Americans, fighting on the wrong side.

> RONALD REAGAN, *using an analogy between the Spanish Civil War and the anti-Sandinista contras in Nicaragua in*

1984. *A 1937 poll showed 65 percent of Americans supported the 3,000 Americans who attempted to defend the Spanish government; a 1938 poll showed 76 percent support.*

They [South Africa] have eliminated the segregation that we once had in our own country—the type of thing where hotels and restaurants and places of entertainment and so forth were segregated—that has all been eliminated.

> RONALD REAGAN *in 1985. A relaxation of South Africa's notorious pass laws did not begin until the early 1990s.*

They are the moral equivalent of our Founding Fathers.

> RONALD REAGAN's *description of the U.S.-backed contra rebels attempting to overthrow the government of Nicaragua, in 1985*

Tell me, General, how dead is the Dead Sea?

> *Vice President* GEORGE BUSH *really did ask Jordanian chief of staff Zeid Bin Shaker this question. Dan Quayle, by contrast, did not, during a trip to Latin America, tell locals he wished he had studied Latin in his youth so that he would be able to speak fluently with them. This was a joke started by Democratic congresswoman Patricia Schroeder that simply sounded so Quaylesque that Quayle's handlers weren't able to squelch it, even after Schroeder apologized for the remark.*

We love your adherence to the democratic principle and to the democratic process.

> *Vice President* GEORGE BUSH *in 1981, during a state visit to the Philippines, where he complimented Ferdinand Marcos on his handling of the country*

A bunch of no-good bums.

> *President* RONALD REAGAN'*s assessment of the Polish government in 1982, during a sound check prior to a national radio address*

You know, your nose looks just like Danny Thomas's.

> RONALD REAGAN *in 1982, to the Lebanese foreign minister during a meeting of Arab leaders at the White House*

Oh, yes. They gave us a boy to play tennis with.

> GEORGE BUSH, *asked if he had mixed with local people during his 16 months as U.S. envoy to China*

Boy, they were big on crematoriums, weren't they?

> *Vice President* GEORGE BUSH *in 1987, after a visit to the Auschwitz death camp*

Deep doo-doo.

> *Vice President* GEORGE BUSH, *returning home from a 1985 visit to China, reporting that some Chinese leaders were doing things that might previously have gotten them into trouble—or "deep doo-doo," as he put it*

Even with all the tanks and gunships from the Soviet Union, my guess is that the Sandinistas would make it about as far as the shopping center in Pecos before Roger Staubach came out of retirement, teamed up with some off-duty Texas Rangers and the front four of the Dallas Cowboys and pushed the Sandinistas down the river, out across the Gulf and right back to Havana where they belong.

> RONALD REAGAN *in 1986, who, despite his confidence in America's ability to thwart Sandinista designs on annexing U.S. territory, continued to press for congressional funding of the anti-Sandinista contras*

The question is, how many relatives does he have in Iowa? That's the only thing I want to know.

> *Presidential candidate* GEORGE BUSH *in 1987, after posing for pictures with Lech Walesa in Warsaw. The hunt for Bush supporters in distant places was understandable; Bush placed a miserable third in the Iowa caucuses.*

Will I lose any aid if we talk?

> JOSE NAPOLEON DUARTE, *president of El Salvador, when asked in 1988 by visitors from South Dakota what advice he might give the United States in handling Panamanian leader Manuel Noriega*

Oh boy, just for that careless remark they'll go wild about Reagan wants to lie to Congress or something.

> RONALD REAGAN *to Israeli prime minister Yitzhak Shamir in 1988,*
> *after telling reporters that the only crime committed by former*
> *national security adviser Robert McFarlane during the Iran-contra*
> *affair was "not telling Congress everything it wanted to know," to*
> *which he added, "I've done that myself."*

Smile.

> ELIZABETH II's *instructions to George Bush during a photo*
> *opportunity at Buckingham Palace in 1989*

Don't drop them.

> ELIZABETH II's *instructions to Ronald Reagan in 1989, on presenting*
> *him with the insignia of his new knighthood*

In the 1960s and 1970s, there were many student movements and turmoils in the United States. Did they have any other recourse but to mobilize police and troops, arrest people and shed blood?

> *Chinese leader* DENG XIAOPING *in 1989, shortly after the*
> *Tiananmen Square massacre*

◆

The public good requires us to betray, and to lie, and to massacre; let us resign this commission to those who are more pliable, and more obedient.

MONTAIGNE

I'm hungry. I was very stupid and talked all the time during the lunch instead of eating.

> *Polish leader* LECH WALESA *in 1989, after hosting George and Barbara Bush at his home in Gdansk*

I can tell you a lot about him, but I don't know whether any of it is true.

> CIA *director* WILLIAM WEBSTER *in 1989, when asked about terrorist Abu Nidal*

C'est fine pour moi.

> GEORGE BUSH *obliging Brian Mulroney's request that he accept one last question at a 1989 press conference in Ottawa*

Far from being a "congressional junket," this trip will take us to areas which I believe we need to visit to understand the dimensions of the problems confronting U.S. national security and to meet the responsibilities we face as members of the subcommittee on defense.

> *Senator* DANIEL INOUYE *in 1989, describing the itinerary of a six-nation tour by senators of Europe and the Mediterranean—with "visits to museums, art galleries, and religious and historical sites," and with wives invited because of "certain responsibilities of protocol and diplomacy."*

When you're dealing with the Middle East, 2,000 years is the normal wait for things to happen.

> *White House spokesman* MARLIN FITZWATER *in 1989, on complaints about the administration's laggard progress in bringing change to the region*

---- ◆ ----

We conferred endlessly and futilely, and arrived at the place
from which we started. Then we did what we knew we had to
do in the first place, and we failed as we knew we would.

WINSTON CHURCHILL

Nelson Mandela is no Martin Luther King. He is more like H. Rap Brown or Willie Horton. His wife, Winnie, has given a new meaning to the word necklace.

Congressman WILLIAM DANNEMEYER *in 1990, decrying*
an invitation to Mandela to address a joint session of
Congress as a "national disgrace." The practice of
"necklacing" in South Africa occurs when a person is
bound up, placed inside a pile of tires, and burned to death
when the tires are set on fire.

Does Mike Tyson live near here?

NELSON MANDELA *in 1990, during a walking tour of*
Manhattan after reporters asked if he had any questions
about the city

This is a delightful surprise to the extent that it is a surprise and it is only a surprise to the extent that we anticipated.

Secretary of State JAMES BAKER *in 1990, on the agreement*
between German chancellor Helmut Kohl and
Soviet president Mikhail Gorbachev on a deal to
reunite Germany

Everybody over there should know that the telephone number is 1-202-456-1414. When you're serious about peace, call us.

> *Secretary of State* JAMES BAKER *in 1990, giving the White House phone number to Israeli conservatives*

No one wants to go back to their district and say that taxes are going up. That's why I'm in Hong Kong.

> *Congressman* ESTEBAN TORRES *of California in 1990, on his tour of Asia during the congressional summer recess*

Anybody that thinks that Japan is going to export democracy to China must be smoking pot.

> RICHARD NIXON *in 1990, on why the United States should take the lead role in promoting human rights in China*

They're running away from communism toward our way of life because of television and basketball. You play basketball in this country for a month, you go back, you're never going to be happy waiting on line for a potato.

> *New York governor* MARIO CUOMO *in 1990, on the collapse of the Soviet Union*

At the turning points of history the scum of the earth come to the surface.

> AGIM LEKA, *an Albanian Communist party official, comments on the anti-Communist protesters who toppled statues and damaged buildings in many cities in 1991*

It was 95 percent ego and 5 percent patriotism, I think.

> ROBERT STRAUSS *on why he accepted the post of U.S. ambassador to Moscow in 1991*

What we're saying is, "Hey, let's forget that, let's go forward now together." And if you see some ugliness in our country about the Japanese, I'll be out front saying, "Hey, knock that off."

> GEORGE BUSH *in 1991, trying to suppress anti-Japan feelings on the eve of the 50th anniversary of the Japanese attack on Pearl Harbor*

At times the republics remind me of our children when they were growing up and they were teenagers. They thoroughly enjoyed their independence until their laundry got dirty and they had to get their laundry done.

> ROBERT STRAUSS, *newly appointed U.S. ambassador to Moscow, on the aspirations of the former union's breakaway republics, in 1991*

You no buy our rice, we no buy your cars.

> *Presidential candidate* DAVID DUKE *in 1991, issuing a bilingual warning to the Japanese. Duke later said, "I just used phraseology for some people who speak broken English."*

---- ◆ ----

He knows nothing and thinks he knows everything. That points clearly to a political career.

> GEORGE BERNARD SHAW, *Major Barbara*

I'm a man that knows every hand gesture you've ever seen—and I haven't learned a new one since I've been here.

> GEORGE BUSH *on a state visit to Australia in 1992. The day after making this comment, the president gave the V-for-victory sign as his motorcade traveled past demonstrators in Canberra, the Australian capital. In Australia, holding up two fingers to form a "V" has the same meaning as the middle-finger salute does in the United States.*

[He's a] 85-year-old chain-smoking Communist dwarf.

> *Presidential candidate* PATRICK BUCHANAN *in 1992, on Chinese leader Deng Xiaoping*

I'd like a loan because it cost a lot to dry-clean a suit over there in Japan and the prime minister had a nice expensive one.

> GEORGE BUSH *campaigning in New Hampshire in 1992, a few days after a state visit to Japan during which he had been sick on Japanese prime minister Kiichi Miyazawa*

The Red Menace

Now, just the other day, one among you . . . has quoted from the Ten Commandments of Nikolai Lenin, that he'd printed as the ten principles—guiding principles of Communism.

> *President* RONALD REAGAN *during a 1982 press conference. Vladimir Ilyich Lenin, the Communist leader to whom he was apparently referring, did not enshrine his philosophy in the form of 10 commandments or principles.*

My fellow Americans, I am pleased to tell you that I've signed legislation that will outlaw Russia forever. We begin bombing in five minutes.

RONALD REAGAN *prior to a 1984 radio interview, speaking into a mike he didn't realize was turned on*

◆

The whole aim of practical politics is to keep the populace alarmed (and hence clamorous to be led to safety) by menacing it with an endless series of hobgoblins, all of them imaginary.
P. J. O'ROURKE in *Parliament of Whores*

I'm no linguist, but I have been told that in the Russian language there isn't even a word for freedom.

RONALD REAGAN *in 1985. The Russian word for freedom is svoboda.*

It's too bad it didn't happen closer to the Kremlin.

Republican senator STEVEN SYMMS *of Idaho, responding to a different drummer while others were expressing sympathy for victims of the Chernobyl accident in 1986*

Mistaken Identities

I'm the Prime Minister of Canada, I live here and I'm about to go and have a leak.

LESTER PEARSON *in 1967, during a meeting between Pearson and President Johnson, whose Secret Service detail had taken over Pearson's cottage retreat. At one point, a Johnson guard asked Pearson: "Who are you and where are you going?"*

Every member of this company feels a very definite sense of honor and distinction in the privilege of having with us tonight the Prime Minister of the Great Republic of Canada.

DWIGHT EISENHOWER *addressing Canadian prime minister John Diefenbaker at a White House dinner in 1960. The United States and France are republics; Britain, Canada, and Australia are constitutional monarchies.*

Mr. Wilson, I want to show you Texas.

LYNDON JOHNSON, *welcoming Canadian prime minister Lester Pearson to his Texas ranch in 1965. He was likely confusing Pearson with British prime minister Harold Wilson. LBJ later called Pearson in Ottawa to apologize. "Think nothing of it, Senator Goldwater," Pearson replied.*

The people of Bolivia.

President RONALD REAGAN *in 1982 during a state visit to Brazil, inviting everyone to join in a toast to President Joao Gigueiredo and his people. Realizing his mistake, Reagan explained that Bolivia was the next stop on his trip. The next stop was, in fact, Colombia; there were no plans to visit Bolivia.*

Ladies and gentlemen, Chairman Moe of Liberia is our visitor here today, and we're very proud to have him.

> RONALD REAGAN *welcomes Liberian leader Samuel K. Doe to the White House*

It gives me great pleasure to welcome Prime Minister Lee Kuan Yew and Mrs. Yew to Singapore.

> RONALD REAGAN *in 1985, welcoming Mr. and Mrs. Lee (surnames come first for Singapore natives) not to Singapore, but to a state function at the White House*

Nice to see you, Mr. Ambassador.

> RONALD REAGAN *in 1987, welcoming British Labour Party leader Denis Healey. The ambassador, whom he has met, shifts his feet nearby.*

Princess David.

> RONALD REAGAN *welcomes Princess Diana to the United States*

Thanks as well to Secretary of Agriculture John Black for his fine leadership.

> RONALD REAGAN *in 1984, thanking his agriculture secretary John Block*

I talked to Jim Baker who talked to . . . who was it Jimmy talked to, Yanayev? No, not Yanayev. Yakovlev is who we talked to.

GEORGE BUSH, *attempting to sort out the names of putative Soviet leaders during the August 1991 coup attempt against Mikhail Gorbachev*

Distant Reports

He speaks to me as if I were a public meeting.

QUEEN VICTORIA *on British prime minister William Gladstone*

It was only one life. What is one life in the affairs of a state?

BENITO MUSSOLINI, *after running down a child in his car*

I do not resent criticism, even when, for the sake of emphasis, it parts for the time with reality.

WINSTON CHURCHILL *in 1941*

A great man? Why, he's selfish, he's arrogant, he thinks he's the center of the universe. Yes, you're right, he's a great man!

WINSTON CHURCHILL *on Charles de Gaulle*

A transistor salesman.

CHARLES DE GAULLE's *description of Japanese prime minister Hayato Ikeda*

Gaiety is the most outstanding feature of the Soviet Union.

JOSEPH STALIN *in 1935*

How can anyone govern a nation that has 246 different kinds of cheese?

CHARLES DE GAULLE

Biafra? Where's Biafra?

PIERRE TRUDEAU'*s response in 1970 when asked for his reaction*
when Nigeria forcibly reannexed a secessionist Biafra

His Imperial Majesty Haile Selassie I, King of Kings, King of Zion, Invincible Lion of the Seed of Judah, Branch of the Tree of Solomon and Implement of the Holy Trinity.

> *Official title of Ethiopian monarch* HAILE SELASSIE

President for Life, Protector of the People, Maximum Chief of the Revolution, Apostle of National Unity, Benefactor of the Poor, Grand Patron of Commerce and Industry, and Electrifier of Souls.

> *Official title of* FRANCIS "PAPA DOC" DUVALIER, *the Haitian dictator. The last reference is to Duvalier's legalization of voodoo, which was allowed provided that voodoo priests paid performance taxes and conducted their rituals under a portrait of Duvalier.*

Jaws is the warmest, tenderest, lovingest movie of the year. I give it four coconuts.

> *Ugandan dictator* IDI AMIN *in 1975*

---◆---

> *There are some politicians who, if their constituents were cannibals, would promise them missionaries for dinner.*
> H. L. MENCKEN

I'm going to leave this car as property of the nation. But meanwhile I'm going to use it myself.

> *Argentine president* CARLOS MENEM, *making little effort to shake his playboy image by deciding to keep a red Ferrari given to him as a gift by an Italian motorcycle company*

We say to them from the heights of this mountain and from the perspective of thousands of years of history that they are like grasshoppers compared to us.

>*Israeli prime minister YITZHAK SHAMIR in 1988, during the opening ceremonies of a West Bank tourist site, on rioting Palestinians*

I don't know what you're talking about, you silly old bugger.

>*Australian prime minister BOB HAWKE in 1989, to an elderly man who criticized the government over his modest pension payments*

It may be the cock that crows, but it is the hen that lays the eggs.

>MARGARET THATCHER

We have both dressed in green.

>*Nicaraguan leader DANIEL ORTEGA in 1989, searching for an answer to a reporter's question following a meeting with Margaret Thatcher in London as to whether the two leaders had anything in common*

Forgive me for saying so, but no.

>MARGARET THATCHER *in 1989, on the 200th anniversary of the French Revolution, when asked on French television if the event held any message for today's world*

Where's the Bastille?

>*Soviet president MIKHAIL GORBACHEV in 1989, arriving at the site of the long-ago-dismantled Paris prison for a photo opportunity*

I think Comrade Gorbachev is a little nervous about me. Yes, unfortunately I think he has the idea I want his job.

Ousted Politburo member BORIS YELTSIN *in 1989*

It is necessary to form a deterrent force against them and develop a situation whereby, when a rat runs across the street, everybody cries "Kill it!"

JIA ZHIJIE, *governor of the Chinese province of Gansu, commenting in 1989 on pro-democracy demonstrators*

What was said on "Viewpoint" about the most sacred thing— Lenin—is worse than incomprehensible. I do not and do not want to understand such pluralism.

Soviet Central Committee member ALEKSEI MYASNIKOV *in 1989, reacting to a suggestion that Lenin's body finally be buried*

Instead [of having] four maids or three maids in the house, you can have two maids.

Kuwaiti minister of state for cabinet affairs ABDEL RAHMAN AL-AWADI, *on the more egalitarian and less materialistic mood of the country after its liberation from Iraqi occupation in 1991*

If you spend all your money on education you'll end up like Kuwait.

Pakistani minister of state for economic affairs SARDAR ASSEF AHMAD ALI, *promoting his faith in lavish defense spending, in 1991*

I am available to make love with Saddam Hussein to achieve peace in the Middle East.

> ILONA (CICCIOLINA) STALLER, *Italian porn star and member of parliament, in 1990*

---◆---

Politics is not the art of the possible. It consists in choosing between the disastrous and the unpalatable.
> JOHN KENNETH GALBRAITH in 1981

It is clear that Japan is an enemy that is not playing the game and that there is an absolute desire to control the world.

> EDITH CRESSON *in 1990, a few months before becoming prime minister of France*

The majority of those men are homosexual—perhaps not the majority—but in the USA there are already 25 percent of them and in England and Germany it is the same. You cannot imagine it in the history of France.

> *Attributed to* EDITH CRESSON, *prime minister of France, in 1991*

They sit up all night thinking of ways to screw the Americans and Europeans.

> *Former French prime minister* EDITH CRESSON's *estimation of the Japanese economic threat to her country, in 1991*

We have to pursue this subject of fun very seriously if we want to stay competitive in the 21st century.

> GEORGE YEO, *Singapore minister of state for finance and foreign affairs, in 1990, urging citizens of the city-state to put on a smile. In 1992, Singapore reverted to its superhygenic ways of the past 30 years, banning the manufacture and sale of chewing gum because too much of it was marring Singapore's pristine downtown streets.*

Let us not forget we are in the Balkans, where lies and deceit are the highest moral values.

> VIKTOR ZAKELJ, *Socialist Party deputy in Slovenia, addressing the secessionist republic's legislature in 1991*

I hope the sheets have been cleaned.

> *Israeli prime minister* YITZHAK SHAMIR *after he was informed that the bed given to him during a Bulgarian state visit had been slept in by Libyan dictator Muammar Qaddafi, in 1991*

Before Christ came into my life, the realities of the materialistic world had the priority in my daily life.

> *Born-again former Panamanian dictator* MANUEL NORIEGA *in 1991*

The truth is no ugly woman can succeed in politics.

> EDITH CRESSON, *newly installed prime minister of France, in 1991*

Not one woman is elected to a political party position without the explanation being heard that she really got the post because she slept with so-and-so or so-and-so. Unfortunately, that is where we still are.

EDITH CRESSON *in 1991*

In a political party, a woman is always in a state of inferiority. As soon as she gets up to speak, no one listens to her. Men start speaking to each other—it's disgusting.

EDITH CRESSON *in 1991*

Anglo-Saxon men are not interested in women. And this is a problem that needs analysis. I don't know whether it is cultural or biological, but there is something there that isn't working—that's obvious. Moreover, I remember from strolling about in London that men in the streets don't look at you. When you do this in Paris . . . a workman, or indeed any man looks at passing women . . . . For a woman arriving in an Anglo-Saxon country, it is astonishing. She says to herself, "What is the matter?"

EDITH CRESSON *in an interview published in Britain's* Observer *newspaper in 1991, but which first appeared in a 1987 book on powerful women. Cresson, who responded to the furor over the interview by saying she didn't remember giving it, suggested in her published comments that Anglo-Saxon men in Britain, Germany, and America are undersexed and that more than one in four are homosexual. Britain's tabloid* Sun *retorted in an editorial headed "Brittany Fairies" that the French are dirty and cowardly. "If you stay in a hotel in France, the best place to hide your money is under the soap."*

Don't hang noodles from my ears.

> *Soviet president* MIKHAIL GORBACHEV *coining a new expression in responding to the coup leaders of August 1991 who told him he was no longer in power*

A man must live like a great bright flame and burn as brightly as he can. In the end he burns out. But this is better than a mean little flame.

> *Russian president* BORIS YELTSIN, *on his sense of mission*

I wish he were more democratic—it wouldn't hurt him.

> MIKHAIL GORBACHEV, *three days before stepping down as Soviet president in December 1991, on erstwhile Politburo colleague Boris Yeltsin*

Fuck 'em. They didn't vote for us.

> *Attributed to Secretary of State* JAMES BAKER *by New York mayor-turned-journalist Ed Koch in 1992. The Bush administration denied Baker said these words, reportedly directed at Jewish critics of the administration's demand that Israel surrender occupied Palestinian territories in return for U.S. aid.*

You should draw a mushroom cloud and put underneath it, "Made in America by lazy and illiterate Americans and tested in Japan."

> *Senator* ERNEST HOLLINGS *of South Carolina in 1992, fanning the flames of Japanophobia—and responding to a Japanese parliamentarian's statement that many American workers are lazy and illiterate—by describing how nuclear bombs should be labeled, to employees at a roller-bearing plant in Hartsville, South Carolina*

·7·

Media Relations

Avoid any specific discussion of public policy . . . at public meetings.

QUINTUS CICERO

Were it left to me to decide whether we should have a government without newspapers, or newspapers without a government, I should not hesitate a moment to prefer the latter.

THOMAS JEFFERSON *in 1787*

Democracy becomes a government of bullies tempered by editors.

RALPH WALDO EMERSON

Never lose your temper with the press or the public is a major rule of political life.

CHRISTABEL PANKHURST, *Unshackled Woman*

Never believe in anything until it has been officially denied.

OTTO VON BISMARCK

What the proprietorship of these newspapers is aiming at is power, and power without responsibility—the prerogative of the harlot through the ages.

British prime minister STANLEY BALDWIN, referring to UK press
barons Beaverbrook and Rothermere

Why should any man be allowed to buy a printing press and disseminate pernicious opinions calculated to embarrass the government?

VLADIMIR ILICH LENIN in 1920

It is the absolute right of the state to supervise the formation of public opinion.

JOSEPH GOEBBELS

In the city of San Francisco we have drunk to the very dregs of infamy; we have had vile officials, we have had rotten newspapers. But we have nothing so vile, nothing so low, nothing so debased, nothing so infamous in San Francisco as [Los Angeles Times publisher] Harrison Gray Otis. He sits there in senile dementia with gangrene heart and rotting brain, grimacing at every reform, chattering impolitely at all things that are decent, frothing, fuming, violently gibbering, going down to his grave in snarling infamy. He is the one thing that all Californians look at when, in looking at Southern California, they see anything that is disgraceful, depraved, corrupt, crooked and putrescent—that is Harrison Gray Otis.

> HIRAM JOHNSON *in 1910, campaigning for governor of California*

The kiss of death.

> *New York governor* ALFRED E. SMITH *in 1926, on the prospects for his unsuccessful gubernatorial challenger Ogden Mills after learning Mills had been endorsed by William Randolph Hearst*

Someday I hope to meet you. When that happens you'll need a new nose, a lot of beefsteak for black eyes, and perhaps a supporter below.

> *Newly inaugurated president* HARRY TRUMAN, *in a note to* Washington Post *music critic Paul Hume, written moments after he read Hume's unflattering review of his daughter Margaret's singing debut in 1945*

I think "No Comment" is a splendid expression. I am using it again and again. I got it from Sumner Welles.

> WINSTON CHURCHILL *in 1946, to reporters in Washington after meeting with President Truman. Welles had been an undersecretary of state in Franklin Roosevelt's administration.*

You won't have Nixon to kick around anymore, because, gentlemen, this is my last press conference.

> RICHARD NIXON *in 1962, on the morning after his defeat to Edmund "Pat" Brown (father of Jerry Brown) in the California gubernatorial race. Assuming that Nixon had indeed been lost from public life for*

good, ABC five days later broadcast a half-hour "Political Obituary of Richard Nixon" starring, among others, an early Nixon adversary named Alger Hiss.

Some newspapers dispose of their garbage by printing it.
Vice President SPIRO AGNEW

Katie Graham is going to get her teat caught in a big fat wringer.
JOHN MITCHELL, *Richard Nixon's former attorney general and chief of his reelection campaign in 1972, warning a* Washington Post *reporter that the paper's publisher was asking for trouble by pursuing the Watergate story*

No, Mr. President, are you?
CBS correspondent DAN RATHER *at a White House press conference in 1974. Richard Nixon, acutely aware of the favorable attention Rather had garnered with his sharp questions about the Watergate affair, had recognized Rather's raised hand during the conference by asking, "Are you running for something?" Rather was later reprimanded by his network bosses for his supposed lack of respect for the office of president.*

Well, did you do any fornicating this weekend?
RICHARD NIXON *to David Frost, moments before taping an interview in 1976*

The score was five to one in my favor.

President RONALD REAGAN *in 1982, claiming an 80 percent accuracy rating in his responses to reporters' questions and complaining about "all those mistakes you said that I made" in a previous news conference*

You don't tell us how to stage the news, and we don't tell you how to report it.

White House spokesman LARRY SPEAKES *in 1982, in a conversation with reporters*

When they use a proctoscope it's going too far.

Former president RICHARD NIXON *in 1984, conceding that the media have a responsibility to scrutinize the presidency "with a microscope," but other devices are beyond the pale*

Someday we can sit down and I would like to match my accuracy with that of the media and I think I'd come out on top.

RONALD REAGAN *in a 1982 interview with Dan Rather*

Get that whore off that chair.

Attributed to Republican senator STEVEN SYMMS *of Idaho, directed at a female TV reporter who was critical of him in her coverage*

I'd come looking for you with a baseball bat.

Senator ALFONSE D'AMATO *of New York, warning a reporter in 1987 of the consequences of negative coverage of his record*

You know, it's Tension City when you're in there.
> GEORGE BUSH *in 1988, a day after being interviewed by Dan Rather*

Blustering, opportunistic, craven, hopelessly ineffective, all at once.
> THE WASHINGTON POST *on George Bush*

Pontifical power puffs.
> *Senator* ALAN SIMPSON *of New York, attacking the media while coming to Dan Quayle's defense during the 1988 campaign*

There was a flurry, there was a feeding flurry in the water out there. Have you ever seen them when they are just squirming all around feeding in a frenzy? That's exactly what was happening.
> GEORGE BUSH *in 1988, remarking on the barrage of reporters' questions inflicted on his recently announced running mate, Dan Quayle*

You hope the American people are fair. We recognize journalists have to kill somebody each week, and Danny's it.
> ROGER AILES, *media consultant to George Bush's 1988 presidential campaign, responding to the negative press reports about Quayle that appeared within days of his selection as Bush's running mate*

What a dog. What a dog. What a stupid dog.
> *New York mayor* ED KOCH *in 1988, complaining about a line of questioning by ABC News reporter Sam Donaldson*

Is it always like this?

> *A reporter for the official Soviet newspaper* Izvestia *while listening to New York mayor Ed Koch lecture Soviet visitors to New York city hall about rehabilitating Leon Trotsky, in 1988*

Reagan is a simple man, a normal man. He likes astrology; maybe he eats spinach; he was an actor. We see this normal man and we want to have a normal man as the leader of our state.

> VITALY KOROTICH, *editor of the Soviet weekly* Ogonyok, *after interviewing President Reagan in 1988*

In a general way, we try to anticipate some of your questions so that I can respond "no comment" with some degree of knowledge.

> WILLIAM BAKER, *a spokesman for the Central Intelligence Agency, explaining in 1988 why the CIA recently completed a study of presidential candidate George Bush's tenure as head of the agency*

It's [presidential candidate Robert] Dole's misfortune that when he does smile, he looks as if he's just evicted a widow.

> *Columnist* MIKE ROYKO *in 1988*

You've done everything but call me a liar. You said that I was cute. You said that I misplayed the game. You said that I was really waiting for another scenario. It really comes down to my credibility or yours.

> *New York governor* MARIO CUOMO *in 1988, urging the media to report his sincerity in rejecting hidden designs to seek the presidency*

Keep the press off the plane.
>Senator ROBERT DOLE, AFTER *withdrawing his candidacy*
>*for the presidency in 1988, when asked how he would have*
>*run his campaign differently*

I think Owen made some of it up. I think he made it up about the dogs, didn't you, Owen?
>*White House press secretary* MARLIN FITZWATER *in 1989, on a story*
>*by reporter Owen Ullman that quoted Bush aides saying Ronald*
>*Reagan's dog Rex was not as well mannered as the Bush dog Millie*

Do you pledge that you and your fellow journalists will continue to demand that all politicians get no pay raise, reveal their income and stop taking honoraria—while steadfastly, sanctimoniously refusing to do any of those things yourselves?
>Senator JOHN GLENN *of Ohio in 1989, swearing in the new president*
>*of the National Press Club*

◆

When reporters come around looking for war stories, the only advice I can give you is the same advice Richard Nixon gave to John Dean: "Don't ever lie, John, but you can always say, 'I can't recall.'"

> Presidential candidate and former Nixon speechwriter PATRICK BUCHANAN in 1992, counseling friends from his youth on how to respond when questioned about tales of Buchanan's combative style at home and in school

---

You have black reporters who are turncoats who just throw themselves out there to be used. In the case of the women, they are Aunt Jemimas.

> Detroit mayor COLEMAN YOUNG, *who is black, in 1989, on his treatment by the Detroit press*

Of course, if a member of the house shouts an obscenity, I put it on the record. But I've had my note pad taken, and one stenographer lost a front tooth to a flying ashtray.

> MIZUNO GORO, *note-taker in the Japanese parliament, explaining the dangers of recording Diet sessions*

Don't tempt me.

> GEORGE BUSH *in 1989, when reporters asked him to display the middle finger from which he was about to have a cyst removed*

These things can be treacherous if you . . .

> GEORGE BUSH *in 1990, fiddling with a microphone moments before*
> *the sound went dead*

Shelly, you're on. Your big moment. Address yourself to Dan Rather, wherever he may be.

> GEORGE BUSH *in 1990, to a woman he met*
> *while touring an Ohio family center, and not realizing*
> *the mike he was wearing was turned on*

Have you stopped wearing your wife's lingerie? Have you stopped messing around with little boys?

> *Illinois congressman* GUS SAVAGE *in 1990, responding to reporters'*
> *questions about sex*

I don't talk to you white motherfuckers . . . you bitch motherfuckers in the white press. . . . Fuck you, you motherfucking assholes.

> *Congressman* GUS SAVAGE *at a reporter with the* Washington
> Times *who tried to interview him*

They made an animal-type grunting sound when the National Guard was mentioned. There were some good-natured grunts. Let me admit theoretically that some people hissed.

> DAVID BECKWITH, *press secretary to Dan Quayle,*
> *in 1989, when asked about reports that the vice*
> *president had been ill-received by cadets during an*
> *appearance at the West Point commencement*

This strategy represents our policy for all time. Until it's changed.

White House spokesman MARLIN FITZWATER *in 1990, explaining to reporters the Bush administration's national security policy*

Who'd you sleep with to get your job?

JON PECK, *press secretary to Florida governor Bob Martinez, to a female* Miami Herald *reporter*

Unidentified blonde!

Senator EDWARD KENNEDY *of Massachusetts in 1990 to paparazzi as he strolled past them with an attractive woman, who turned out to be his sister Jean Kennedy Smith*

I do mind being described as flaky, particularly by somebody like [*New Republic* magazine] writer Fred Barnes, who makes a living being flaky.

Presidential candidate BOB KERREY *in 1991*

We just don't discuss that capability. I can't tell you why we don't discuss it because then I'd be discussing it.

Defense department spokesman PETE WILLIAMS *in 1991, deflecting questions about the use of missiles in the Persian Gulf war*

They've been operating jointly on me for years.

Detroit mayor COLEMAN YOUNG *in 1991, on the outcome of a bid by the* Detroit Free Press *and* The Detroit News *to win federal approval of a joint*

operating agreement—a type of merger designed to
save the money-losing papers from insolvency

I left Holland as a kid in 1947 and I guess we got away from
oppression and this is all very reminiscent of Nazi Germany.
British Columbia premier WILLIAM VANDER ZALM *in 1991, equating*
allegations of conflict of interest directed at him and the climate of
persecution in wartime Europe

I might start by recommending that you put "Doonesbury" in the
obituary section; that might make a contribution.
GEORGE BUSH in 1991, responding to a question at a convention of
newspaper publishers about how the economy could be improved. At
the time, the comic strip was dealing with widely dismissed allegations
of drug use by Vice President Quayle.

---- ◆ ----

To err is human. To blame someone else is politics.
HUBERT HUMPHREY

That's the kind of cheap shot a little worm like you would make. . . .
You could use a little plastic surgery yourself.
DAVID DUKE, candidate for Louisiana governor, responding to CNN
commentator Michael Kinsley's question about whether Duke had
ever had a chemical face peel, in 1991

In this campaign, I have been called an anti-Semite, a homophobe, a racist, a sexist, a nativist, a protectionist, an isolationist, a social fascist and a beer-hall conservative. And then Sam Donaldson had the nerve on the Brinkley show to ask me if I was insensitive, too. I am none of the above.

Presidential candidate PATRICK BUCHANAN *in 1992*

A barbed-wire enema.

Presidential candidate PATRICK BUCHANAN *in 1992, characterizing the media assessments of his message*

·8·

First Ladies and Gentlemen

Topping is just not on. Go around topping people and it always comes back to you in the end.

> DENIS THATCHER, *husband of British prime minister Margaret Thatcher, chastising Pakistani dictator General Zia ul-Haq for his regime's 1979 execution of Zulfikar Ali Bhutto, the country's first democratically elected prime minister. In 1988, Zia died in a mysterious plane crash. "Topping," in the parlance of the private clubs to which Denis Thatcher belongs, is a politic expression for murdering one's foes.*

One a day is enough.

> DENIS THATCHER *in 1989, asked by reporters to reenact a kiss on the hand given by him to Barbara Bush during a state visit by the First Couple*

Behind every successful man stands a surprised woman.
> *Attributed to* MARYON PEARSON, *wife of Canadian prime minister*
> *Lester Pearson*

———————————— ♦ ————————————

Behind every so-so candidate is a smart woman who makes
him look good because he was savvy enough to marry her.
> ANNA QUINDLEN, *columnist for*
> The New York Times

Yes, about twelve cups of coffee and eight donuts.
> MARYON PEARSON, *asked at the end of a day of campaigning with her*
> *husband if the couple "had anything else to bring up"*

We've lost everything. We even won our seat.
> MARYON PEARSON, *who did not enjoy public life, bemoaning how she*
> *and her husband would have to remain in the political sphere even*
> *though his party had lost the 1957 election*

The big problem is to find suitable hats. I don't care for them all that
much, but you have to wear them in politics.

> MARYON PEARSON

Welcome to Liberace and to the Prime Minister.
> *Sign outside a London, Ontario hotel where Lester Pearson was*
> *making a 1965 appearance. After wife Maryon joked to her husband,*

*"Second fiddle to a piano player," the sign was changed to read,
"Welcome to Mrs. Pearson and husband."*

I feel they're frittering away hours in meaningless haranguing when they should be getting important things accomplished.

> MARYON PEARSON, *on the quality of parliamentary debate*

Men are strange about politics. I have been around the world twice and know politicians from many cultures. They are all alike. As long as they find themselves in the middle of it, they say they are sorry that all their time is taken up by politics. But as soon as they have lost and are out—oh, how terrible for them!

> MARYON PEARSON *in a 1962 interview*

I sometimes found myself surveying the table with loathing and irritation: what in the world can I possibly find to talk to these crows about?

> MARGARET TRUDEAU, *estranged wife of Canadian prime minister
> Pierre Trudeau, in her autobiography* Beyond Reason, *on the trials
> of making small talk with the wives of visiting delegations*

We are so much alike. Don't you think we could have a beautiful chocolate-colored daughter together?

> MARGARET TRUDEAU *to Lou Rawls in 1979*

Anyone who knows Dan Quayle knows he would rather play golf than have sex any day.

> MARILYN QUAYLE, *wife of Indiana senator Dan Quayle, responding
> to a 1981 gossip-column item about his golfing weekend with a few*

other federal legislators at a Florida vacation home in the company of
Playboy model Paula Parkinson, who claimed to have videotaped
several congressmen in her bedroom. Dan Quayle said he didn't
"remember anyone by the name of Paula Parkinson."

Beauty is love made real, and the spirit of love is God. And the state of beauty, love; and God is happiness. A transcendent state of beauty, love, and God is peace. Peace and love is a state of beauty, love, and God. One is an active state of happiness, and the other is a transcendent state. That's peace.

IMELDA MARCOS, *campaigning for husband Ferdinand Marcos in 1986*

Everybody kept their shoes there. The maids . . . everybody.

IMELDA MARCOS *in 1986, after her hasty departure from the Philippines with her husband, and the revelations about her massive footwear collection*

Our beautiful Hawaiian isle is, for us, worse than Alcatraz. Alcatraz at least gives free room and board.

IMELDA MARCOS *in 1988, on the difficulties of life in exile*

I guess the biggest shock to me was all these people saying you cannot have two strong people together—if the woman is strong, the man is weak. The reality is that to have a strong woman, you need a very strong man.

MAUREEN MCTEER, *wife of Canadian prime minister Joe Clark,*

responing to late-1970s criticism over her decision to retain her
maiden name after their marriage

I didn't have time to do my hair.

> MICHELE DUVALIER, *"Baby Doc's" wife, on leaving Haiti for
> good in 1986*

Okay, Mr. Environmentalist, come here and explain this.

> LUCINDA FLORIO, *wife of New Jersey governor Jim Florio, in
> 1990, on discovering that the faucets in the governor's mansion emit
> brown water*

I know my role and I know my limitations. What I do within those
limitations, that's up to me. I have always been very accountable for
everything I say.

> MILA MULRONEY, *wife of Canadian prime minister Brian Mulroney,
> in 1986*

I do sinks, I do all that, absolutely. . . . And my husband does a lot of
things. Brian rinses out his tub, he certainly does. There's a certain
knowledge that one day all this is going to be over and there's going to
be him and me and we'll have a little apartment.

> MILA MULRONEY *in 1984*

He could pick up his clothes a little more.

> MARILYN QUAYLE *in 1991, on how she might change husband
> Dan Quayle*

The Nancy Reagan Reign

Nancy knows not only her own lines but everybody else's. She picks up the cue her terrified classmates forget to give, improvises speeches for all and sundry. Just a part of the game for Nancy.

> *Description of Nancy Reagan in her 1939 high school yearbook, on her lead role in her senior class play*, First Lady

Ronnie was away a lot, you know, and I was alone in that house. . . . It's just a tiny little gun.

> NANCY REAGAN *in 1980, explaining why she keeps a gun in her bedside table*

The White House really badly, badly needs china.

> *Newly inaugurated First Lady* NANCY REAGAN, *explaining why in her first year on the job—the recession year of 1981—she ordered $200,000 worth of new china for the presidential mansion*

Now that's silly. I would never wear a crown. It messes up your hair.

> NANCY REAGAN *in a speech at a New York fund-raiser, alluding to a popular satirical postcard depicting the First Lady as "Queen Nancy," dressed in royal garb and wearing a crown*

I think people would be alive today if there were a death penalty.

> NANCY REAGAN *in 1981*

I don't think most people associate me with leeches or how to get them off. But I know how to get them off. I'm an expert at it.

> NANCY REAGAN *a few days after the forced departure of arch-enemy Donald Regan from the post of White House chief of staff. A few months earlier, talk-show host Joan Rivers had told her guest Nancy Reagan, "There's such warmth coming out of you, it's incredible!"*

It didn't help when Mike tried to explain it by telling Chris Wallace of NBC that Ronnie occasionally nodded off during Cabinet meetings! Actually, everyone at one time or another had a hard time keeping his eyes open at Cabinet meetings.

> NANCY REAGAN, *recalling an error in judgment by Reagan aide Michael Deaver in responding to questions about photographs of Reagan nodding off during a public meeting with the Pope at the Vatican in 1982. Acknowledging her embarrassment during the incident, Nancy said she wished the Pope, noticing that Reagan was drifting off, "would lean over, nudge Ronnie and say, 'You know what I mean, Ron.'"*

I'm trying not to do it as much as I have done it in the past.

> NANCY REAGAN *in 1985, on what had become known as "The Gaze"—her way of staring at her husband with adoration whenever he spoke in public*

A woman is like a teabag—only in hot water do you realize how strong she is.

Nancy Reagan

Nancy to Ron on Election Day 1980, when her husband was asked what his prospects for victory were: Cautiously optimistic.
Ron to reporters: Yes, I'm cautiously optimistic.
Nancy to Ron: Doing everything we can.
Ron to reporters: We're doing everything we can.

Nancy Reagan *in 1984, prompting her husband during a press scrum*

I can't say it's an award I dreamed of getting when I was growing up.

Nancy Reagan *in 1988, on accepting a White House Cancer Courage award*

I really tried . . . I really tried not to be vindictive or mean.

> NANCY REAGAN *in 1989, on her just-published autobiography,* My Turn, *in which she found manifest fault with former presidential chief of staff Don Regan, Soviet First Lady Raisa Gorbachev, and others*

As much as I love Ronnie, he does have at least one fault that I'll admit to: he can be naive about the people around him.

> NANCY REAGAN *in* My Turn, *referring to presidential counselors who traded arms for hostages, breached conflict-of-interest rules, admitted in public that supply-side economics was a "Trojan horse" designed to enrich the rich at the expense of others, spread rumors about Nancy's habit of forgetting to return garments borrowed from couturiers, overbooked Ronnie to the point of exhaustion so that he couldn't help but fall asleep during Papal audiences, rejected the advice of his own wife and her astrologer about the morale-sapping activities of Don Regan. . . .*

I make no apologies for telling [Ronald Reagan] what I thought. For eight years I was sleeping with the President, and if that doesn't give you special access, I don't know what does!

> NANCY REAGAN *in* My Turn

Well, ask her the next time you see her, please ask if she knows a good Filipino couple—for Ronnie and me—when we retire to California.

> NANCY REAGAN *to a friend of Imelda Marcos in 1988, as reported by columnist Liz Smith*

The Barbara Bush Years

I won't say the word, but it rhymes with rich.

> BARBARA BUSH, *wife of vice-presidential candidate*
> *George Bush, criticizing Geraldine Ferraro's bid to*
> *play up her modest ethnic background in her campaign*
> *as Walter Mondale's running mate in 1984. Barbara later*
> *called Ferraro to apologize, and told reporters the word*
> *she had in mind was "witch," not "bitch."*

Please don't take any pictures of me swimming—my children are complaining all across the country.

> BARBARA BUSH *in 1988, after saying she'd gained 13 pounds on the*
> *campaign trail*

I am a liberal.

> BARBARA BUSH *in 1989, about a year after her husband was*
> *elected on a liberal-bashing platform, describing her own views on*
> *social issues*

You know, down in Texas we call people like that "fat A's."

> BARBARA BUSH *in 1989, after a White House guest broke a dining*
> *table by sitting on it*

Joy.

> BARBARA BUSH *in 1990, on what she meant when she said former*
> *New York mayor Ed Koch was "full of it"*

Instead, you got me, known for the color of my hair.

> BARBARA BUSH *in a commencement speech at Wellesley College in Massachusetts in 1990, acknowledging that she was the second-choice speaker after Alice Walker, author of* The Color Purple

I rarely hug guns.

> BARBARA BUSH, *wife of NRA member George Bush, flinching in 1990 at a combat rifle handed to her for inspection during a photo opportunity in the Saudi desert during the Persian Gulf war*

We do have a little trouble competing with Versailles and places like that.

> BARBARA BUSH *in 1990, on the task of hosting the Group of Seven summit in Houston*

I am looking at a picture of you . . . depicted on a plastic cup . . . with your blue hair filled with pink birds peeking out all over. Evidently, you and your charming family—Lisa, Homer, Bart and Maggie—are camping out. It's a nice family scene. Clearly you are setting a good example for the rest of the country.

> BARBARA BUSH *in a 1990 letter to cartoon character Marge Simpson*

You are so sweet, but you are so ugly. You have a pig's nose, you are bow-legged, and your eyes are yellow.

> BARBARA BUSH *in conversation with White House dog Millie as recorded in the 1990 book,* Millie's Book: As Dictated to Barbara Bush

He was the handsomest-looking man you ever laid your eyes on, bar none. I mean, my boys don't even come close to him, nor did his own brothers. I really like him very much.

BARBARA BUSH *on her husband*

♦

We like you! But you're sleeping with the enemy.
Message on a placard held by a protester who greeted Barbara Bush when she campaigned for her husband in the New Hampshire primary in 1992

The difference between Nancy and me is—and it's a sad one on my part—she didn't eat when she worried. Not me. I eat my way right through a crisis.

BARBARA BUSH *in 1990, on a distinction between herself and former First Lady Nancy Reagan*

Anyone who eats pork rinds can't be all good.

BARBARA BUSH *in 1990, asserting her pro-broccoli stand, on her husband, who in a moment of affected populism during the 1988 presidential race confessed his fondness for pork rinds*

You may think the President is all-powerful, but he is not. He needs a lot of guidance from the Lord.

BARBARA BUSH *in 1991*

Former Lives of First Husbands

Maybe if I hadn't been so fastidious, I might have changed history. But, oh, that body odor of his.

> LINA BASQUETTE, *former silent-film star, telling an interviewer in 1991 why she did not let Adolf Hitler seduce her*

[Sex is best] in the afternoon, after coming out of the shower.

> *Attributed to* RONALD REAGAN *by actress Viveca Lindfors, who claimed in 1981 that he had made this observation to her*

I'm saying, "Listen, stop. That's not what I want." He was really forceful. You know he's very tall, very strong. I was very lightweight. It was just a battle that, I'm sorry to say, I lost. It was absolutely against my will and it was all over in two minutes.

> SELENE WALTERS, *former Hollywood starlet, describing in 1991 a sexual encounter with Ronald Reagan that took place around 1951*

I'm not as seductive as it seems.

> *Argentine president* CARLOS SAUL MENEM *in 1990, on his reputation as a womanizer*

Men About the House

The man who accompanied Jackie to Poland.

> JOHN F. KENNEDY'*s self-description after a state visit by the First Couple to Poland*

Her judgment, which is partly based on gut, partly on intuition, partly on reflex, is remarkable. Absolutely remarkable. For people, for issues, for political solutions. Just amazing. It's a good thing people don't know how influential she is.

> BRIAN MULRONEY *on his wife Mila*

[Our son] Nicholas got lost in our shoe closet and it took us an hour to find him.

> BRIAN MULRONEY *speaking at a Parliamentary Press Gallery dinner at the height of "Guccigate," when it was revealed that Mulroney and his wife had borrowed $300,000 in Progressive Conservative Party funds to renovate the prime minister's official residence, using some of the money to build closets large enough to hold some 50 pairs of Gucci shoes*

She's from the South. She's a woman. And . . . she's a Dole.

> *Senator* ROBERT DOLE *in 1988, enumerating wife Elizabeth Dole's qualifications to be selected as George Bush's presidential running mate*

It would be all right with me. I'd probably get a car and driver out of it.

> *Senator* ROBERT DOLE *in 1988, on the outcome if his wife were to be selected as Bush's running mate*

She is my echo chamber.

> RONALD REAGAN *on his wife Nancy*

Look, you don't talk to your boss about your boss's wife. I mean, do you go in and discuss with your boss what his wife is doing? No, you don't. Now admit it. Give me a break here.

> DON REGAN, *President Reagan's ousted chief of staff, on why he didn't confront Nancy Reagan about her use of an astrologer*

I don't understand it and it doesn't interest me.

> *Senator* GORDON "GORDO" HUMPHREY *of New Hampshire, commenting on his wife Patricia's work in creating a national organization devoted to orgonomy, a field of psychology that holds that orgasms are essential to mental health*

I don't know if it has an "e."

> *California congressman* PETE STARK, 60, *when asked the spelling of the name of his fiancée, 24-year-old Deborah Ann (without an "e") Roderick, in 1991*

Everybody's talking about where's Barbara, we miss her very, very much. And I told her I didn't need her here, I was not going to throw up.

> GEORGE BUSH *on a campaign swing through New Hampshire in January 1992, a few days after he had been sick to his stomach on the Japanese prime minister during a state visit to Japan*

With all the high expectations for this speech, I wanted it to be a big hit. But I couldn't convince Barbara to deliver it.

> GEORGE BUSH's *introductory remark before delivering his State of the Union address to Congress in 1992*

If the wife comes through as being too strong and too intelligent, it makes the husband look like a wimp.

> RICHARD NIXON *in 1992, warning Democratic presidential hopeful*
> *Bill Clinton to be careful in not letting his wife Hillary play too*
> *dominant a role in Clinton's campaign. Nixon said many voters*
> *concur with Cardinal de Richelieu's assertion that, "Intellect in a*
> *woman is unbecoming."*

·9·

Quayludes

In His Own Words

AUH20

> License plate borne by Dan Quayle's sports car in the early 1960s.
> The code is the chemical symbol for gold and water. Barry Goldwater
> was one of Quayle's earliest heroes.

Chief grave robber of my state.

> DAN QUAYLE's dim view of his early political career posting as
> director of Indiana's inheritance-tax division. Among Quayle's
> earliest assignments was his work at the 1968 Republican National
> Convention as a driver for Richard Nixon's aides.

Vietnam-era veteran.

> DAN QUAYLE's self-description in campaign literature during his
> successful 1980 bid to unseat Indiana Senator Birch Bayh. Two days

after George Bush announced his selection of Quayle as his running mate, the Indianapolis News—*which is owned by the Quayle family—broke the news that one of its own former editors had intervened to get the then-22-year-old Quayle a place in the National Guard, which was never called up for duty in Vietnam. Quayle's six-year stint with the Guard consisted mostly of weekend duty and summer camp and writing press releases while studying for a law degree. During an uneventful stint in the Senate, Quayle chiefly distinguished himself by defending America's participation in the Vietnam conflict and supporting increases in the defense budget.*

Coyn and sorbean.

> DAN QUAYLE *in 1988, on the drought that is affecting corn and soybean crops, during an appearance on "This Week" with David Brinkley*

You know, I'm not so sure that we want all those that graduated number one or number two in their class to be on . . . our federal judiciary. This is a diversified society.

> *Senator* DAN QUAYLE *in 1986, explaining to Ted Koppel why he lobbied furiously to garner support for the appointment of federal judge Daniel Manion, who won Senate confirmation by just one vote*

I do, I do, I do, I do what any normal person would do at that age. You call home. You call home to mother and father and say, "I'd like to get in the National Guard."

> DAN QUAYLE *in 1988, on his war record*

I did not know in 1969 that I'd be in this room today.
>DAN QUAYLE *in 1988, responding to reporters' questions about his*
war record

Another Jimmy Carter grain embargo, Jimmy, Jimmy Carter, Jimmy Carter grain embargo, Jimmy Carter grain embargo.
>DAN QUAYLE, *as the expression has it, "goes ballistic" in*
attempting to ridicule the Democrats' position on grain embargoes.
Spy *magazine drew a comparison to "Sarah Vaughan scatting a line*
to smithereens."

◆

It isn't worth a pitcher of warm piss.
>JOHN NANCE GARNER, vice president during
Franklin Roosevelt's first two terms as president,
describing the post of vice president. At the time he
made the comment, it was tamed to "warm spit" in
press accounts.

I'm Dan Quayle. I'm Dan Quayle. I'm Dan Quayle. I am Dan Quayle. The real Dan Quayle. The real Dan Quayle stand up. I'm Dan Quayle. I'm Dan Quayle.
>DAN QUAYLE *in 1988, in a transcript from an eloquence-training*
session he took soon after being named Bush's running mate

I wish Barry would just say what's on his mind.
>DAN QUAYLE *in 1988, on former Arizona senator Barry Goldwater,*

who had just told Quayle, "I want you to go back and tell George
Bush to start talking about the issues, okay?"

An obscene period in our nation's history.

DAN QUAYLE *in 1988, on the Nazi Holocaust*

I understand that immediately after a rape that is reported, that a woman normally, in fact, can go to the hospital and have a D and C. At that time that is before the forming of a life. That is not anything to do with abortion.

DAN QUAYLE *in 1988, making clear his position on the pro-life argument*

I am the future.

DAN QUAYLE *campaigning in 1988*

The real question for 1988 is whether we're going to go forward to tomorrow or past to the—to the back!

DAN QUAYLE *campaigning in 1988*

Perestroika is nothing more than refined Stalinism.

DAN QUAYLE *campaigning in 1988*

[Republicans] understand the importance of bondage between parent and child.

DAN QUAYLE *in 1988, on bonding between parents and children*

Getting them more accurate so that we can have precise precision.

> DAN QUAYLE *in 1988, explaining that his eight years on the*
> *Senate Armed Services Committee compensate for not seeing action*
> *in Vietnam, and that his duty included ensuring the accuracy of*
> *cruise missiles*

Bobby Knight told me, "There is nothing that a good defense cannot beat a better offense." In other words, a good offense wins.

> DAN QUAYLE *in 1988, confusing his audience at the City*
> *Club of Chicago*

I think, unfortunately, I had to be the target, that this bimbo thing was going to be applied to men someday, and I hate it.

> DAN QUAYLE *in 1988, not long after he said that he had "not live[d]*
> *in this century," suggesting that his image problem had to do with*
> *criticisms that he had been put on the GOP ticket only because he*
> *was a pretty face*

◆

Do candidates now pose for office, rather than run for office?
> HARRY BOYLE, Canadian journalist

You all look like happy campers to me. Happy campers you are. Happy campers you have been. And, as far as I am concerned, happy campers you will always be.

> DAN QUAYLE *addressing a group of dignitaries in Samoa in 1989*

Hawaii has always been a very pivotal role in the Pacific. It is *in* the Pacific. It is a part of the United States that is an island that is right here.

> DAN QUAYLE *in 1989, during a visit to Hawaii*

What a waste it is to lose one's mind—or to not have a mind. How true that is.

> DAN QUAYLE *in 1989, addressing the United Negro College Fund*

The destruction, it just is very heart-rendering.

> DAN QUAYLE *in 1989, assessing the damage after the San Francisco earthquake that year, in an apparent reference to the quake's heart-rending aftermath*

Oh, no, "condemn"—that's why it's on background.

> DAN QUAYLE *in 1989, in an off-the-record session with reporters, after being asked to clarify his statement that America "condones" violence in Latin American countries*

I stand by all the mis-statements.

> DAN QUAYLE *in 1989, on his oratorical slip-ups*

I know John McLaughlin. John McLaughlin is my friend. And you're no John McLaughlin.

> DAN QUAYLE *in 1989, at a roast for columnist Robert Novak*

I could take this home, Marilyn, this is something teenage boys might find of interest.

> DAN QUAYLE *during a 1990 visit to Chile, moments before purchasing a South American Indian doll that, when lifted, displays an erection. Wife Marilyn Quayle, sensing disaster and attempting in vain to ward it off, said, "Dan, you're not getting that. Oh, no."*

Dick and I have something in common. That is that we both overmarried.

> DAN QUAYLE *in 1990, on defense secretary Dick Cheney, who is married to Lynne Cheney, chairman of the National Endowment for the Humanities*

I love California; I grew up in Phoenix.

> DAN QUAYLE *responding to a question about his ability to help the GOP presidential ticket carry California in 1992*

We offer the party as a big tent. How we do that within the platform, the preamble to the platform or whatnot, that remains to be seen. But that message will have to be articulated with great clarity.

> DAN QUAYLE *during a luncheon with journalists, speaking on abortion. This comment earned Quayle a Golden Bull award from the British-based Plain English Campaign, which noted that this was the first instance in the Campaign's 13-year history that an American had been honored with one of its annual citations for incomprehensible remarks.*

P.S.: Have you decided yet?

> DAN QUAYLE *in a footnote to his 1991 letter of apology to New York governor Mario Cuomo, whom he had taken to calling by his first name in an effort, Cuomo alleged, to remind Americans of Cuomo's Italian heritage as a means of thwarting a Cuomo presidential bid*

I happen to be a Republican president—ah, the vice-president.

> DAN QUAYLE *in 1990, on his role in the Bush administration*

Make no mistake about it: Operation Desert Storm was a victory of good over evil, of freedom over tyranny, of peace over war.

> DAN QUAYLE *to a Memorial Day audience in 1991*

I love it when I hear the media describe someone 44 years of age as mature and well seasoned.

> DAN QUAYLE *on baseball pitcher Nolan Ryan, in 1991*

You know, I would rather have been a professional golfer, but my family pushed me into politics.

> DAN QUAYLE, *who still finds a lot of time for golf, is known to the Secret Service by the code word, "Scorecard"*

If I had my way no man guilty of golf would be eligible to any office of trust or profit under the United States.

> H. L. MENCKEN

What Others Say About Him

Don't care what they say about you, as long as they respect you.

> *Advice to Quayle from his grandfather* EUGENE PULLIAM

Hello, everybody. I'm Dan Quayle.

> ROBERT REDFORD *in 1988, introducing Michael Dukakis at a New Jersey rally. Quayle had recently been dubbed "the Redford candidate" by the media.*

The Lord gave me faith, the bank loaned me the money, and Dan Quayle gave me JTPA.

> *A Quayle endorsement by Louisiana potato-chip maker* RON ZAPPE *in 1988. Zappe attributed his entrepreneurial success to the federal Joint Training Partnership Act, co-sponsored by Senators Quayle and . . . Edward Kennedy.*

He tries to read Plato's *Republic* every year.

> *An endorsement by wife* MARILYN QUAYLE, *when asked in 1988*
> *about her husband's intellectual attainments*

Franklin Roosevelt was a lousy student. He failed the bar exam seven times.

> MARILYN QUAYLE *in 1988, deflecting questions about her husband's*
> *academic record. FDR passed the bar exam on his first attempt.*

What he learned in golf—the repetition, the practice.

> *A Quayle endorsement from his father,* JAMES QUAYLE, *who was*
> *asked to describe his son's qualifications for public office*

If he's such a hawk, why didn't he choose to go to Vietnam?

> *An endorsement from* ROBERT STEELE, *a high-school and college*
> *classmate of Quayle, in 1988*

I know Dan Quayle, I've served in the Senate with Dan Quayle. Dan Quayle is my friend. And, sir, you're no Dan Quayle.

> *Senator* LLOYD BENTSEN *in 1988, greeting Ohio congressman*
> *Dennis Eckart, who had served as Quayle's stand-in during*
> *Bentsen's vice-presidential debate rehearsals. During*
> *the televised debate, Quayle compared his values favorably with*
> *those of one-time senator John F. Kennedy, eliciting this response*
> *from Bentsen: "I knew Jack Kennedy, I served in the Senate with*
> *Jack Kennedy. Jack Kennedy was my friend. And you, sir, are no*
> *Jack Kennedy."*

He was like a kid. Ask him to turn off a light, and by the time he gets to the switch, he's forgotten what he went for.

Endorsement from former campaign assistant JOE CANZERI *in 1989*

We went to the meeting with low expectations. Like most Americans, we could have drawn up a long list of names of people qualified to be vice president and J. Danforth Quayle wouldn't have been on it. Well, we talked with him Monday. His name still wouldn't be on it.

Editorial in the Charlotte Observer *in 1989*

---◆---

Politics is perhaps the only profession for which no preparation is thought necessary.

ROBERT LOUIS STEVENSON, *Familiar Studies of Men and Books*

As for the look on Dan Quayle's face—how to describe it? Well, let's see. If a tree fell in a forest, and no one was there to hear it, it might sound like Dan Quayle looks.

Television critic Tom Shales in 1990, offering an existential observation after watching the Vice President's expression as he watched President Bush deliver his state of the union address

Take [out] the word "Quayle" and insert the word "Bush" wherever it appears, and that's the crap I took for eight years. Wimp. Sycophant.

Lap dog. Poop. Lightweight. Boob. Squirrel. Asshole. George Bush.

> *Counsel that* GEORGE BUSH *is said to have given Quayle in coping with the rigors of vice-presidential ridicule, according to Senator Alan Simpson in 1992*

There's a price to be paid for democracy. There's Dan Quayle in the United States, and then there's Don Getty.

> *Canadian novelist* MORDECAI RICHLER *in 1992, ridiculing Alberta premier Don Getty's call for an end to official bilingualism in Canada*

·10·

Scandals

Warren, it's a lucky thing you weren't born a girl, because you can't say no.

> President WARREN HARDING, *recalling his father's advice after the Teapot Dome scandal*

It kind of filters down from the top somehow.

> *First Lady–elect* NANCY REAGAN *in 1980, vowing that the incoming First Couple will set an example for "a return to a higher sense of morality" in government. By 1987, 110 senior Reagan appointees had been accused of unethical or illegal conduct—a record unsurpassed in this century, eclipsing even the Nixon White House.*

Mistakes were made.

> RONALD REAGAN'*s bid for contrition after the Iran-contra scandal came to light*

205

[I was] deliberately excluded . . . unaware . . . denied information.

> *Vice President GEORGE BUSH, maintaining that he knew nothing about the arms for hostages deal despite his having attended at least 30 meetings, beginning in 1985, in which the deal was discussed. When an Israeli official publicly mentioned having told Bush that the United States was dealing with radicals, not moderates, in Iran, Bush admitted that he'd known about the arms sales but stated that he had "expressed certain reservations about certain aspects" of U.S. policy. When President Reagan was asked at a news conference on March 19, 1988, whether Bush had objected to the arms deal, he said "No." Secretary of State George Schultz carried the point further: "The Vice President favored the sales."*

The symbolism is, I suspect, manifold.

> *Assistant U.S. attorney general ROBERT MARZULLA in 1988, on retirement presents received by Attorney General Edwin Meese, who was the subject of investigations of alleged violation of government ethics standards at the time. The gifts included a gold-plated hand grenade and a tomahawk.*

I was out of the loop.

> *Vice President GEORGE BUSH, explaining why he knew nothing about the illegal channeling of arms profits to the contras. A White House memo specifically states that the purpose of a May 1, 1986, meeting between Bush and Felix Rodriguez, contra operative and former CIA agent, was "to brief the Vice President on the war in El Salvador and resupply of the contras." In January 1986 Oliver North wrote in his*

notebook "Felix [Rodriguez] talking too much about
VP connection." And on Thanksgiving 1985, Bush wrote
North a handwritten note thanking him "for your work
in Central America."

Justice in the political arena will take a little longer.
> *Impeached governor EVAN MECHAM of Arizona in 1988, celebrating*
> *his acquittal on charges of failing to report a campaign loan, and*
> *hinting he might run for his old job or a seat in Congress*

I'm the luckiest man in the world. The Lord is on my side.
> *Washington mayor MARION BARRY in 1990, in videotaped*
> *comments made moments before FBI agents burst into a hotel room*
> *to arrest him on drug possession charges*

◆

What the mob thirsts for is not good government in itself, but
the merry chase of a definite exponent of bad government.
> H. L. MENCKEN in 1914

That's garbage. Why can't they catch me in a sex scandal? I could use
some good publicity.
> *California assembly speaker WILLIE BROWN in 1990, on an FBI*
> *investigation into his connection with a garbage company*

To forcibly remove a politician from public office, one has to meet a much higher standard of dishonesty.

> MICHAEL COONEY, *Santa Barbara attorney, responding to people demanding the resignation in 1991 of a city councilman who admitted to switching price tags on items he bought from a store*

The Third-Rate Burglary

I want the most comprehensive notes on all those who tried to do us in. They didn't have to do it. . . . They were doing this quite deliberately and they are asking for it and they are going to get it.

> *President* RICHARD NIXON *in a taped Oval Office conversation with aides H. R. (Bob) Haldeman and John Dean in 1972*

Okay, John. Good night. Get a good night's sleep. And don't bug anybody without asking me.

> RICHARD NIXON, *concluding a taped telephone conversation with his former attorney general John Mitchell, who had just stepped down as manager of his reelection campaign, in 1972*

I can say categorically that his investigation indicates that no one in the White House staff, no one in this Administration, presently employed, was involved in this very bizarre incident.

> *President* RICHARD NIXON *in 1972, referring to an inquiry into the Watergate break-in that was being conducted at his request by presidential counsel John Dean. Dean, hearing Nixon's comments on a newscast, was astonished: He had made no investigation, he had not even met with the president to discuss plans for an inquiry.*

What really hurts in matters of this sort is not the fact that they occur, because overzealous people in campaigns do things that are wrong. What hurts is if you try to cover it up.

RICHARD NIXON *on the "Watergate affair," as he usually called it, in 1972. The White House effort to cover up the June 17, 1972, break-in of Democratic Party offices in the Watergate complex began on the morning of June 18.*

◆

You can't adopt politics as a profession and remain honest.
LOUIS MCHENRY HOWE, senior aide to Franklin Roosevelt, in 1933

I am not a crook.

RICHARD NIXON

Don't confuse me with the facts. I've got a closed mind.

Indiana congressman EARL LANDGREBE, a staunch supporter of Richard Nixon, confronted in 1974 by reporters with the so-called "smoking gun" Oval Office tape recording which indicated that the Watergate cover-up had begun with Nixon's knowledge and encouragement

I don't give a shit what happens. I want you all to stonewall it, let them plead the Fifth Amendment, cover up or anything else, if it'll save it, save the plan.

RICHARD NIXON's *comments on how to handle the Watergate affair.*

*Release of this Oval Office recording was followed within a few days
by Nixon's resignation as president.*

Just destroy all the tapes.
> RICHARD NIXON *in 1986, when asked what was the greatest lesson of
> the Watergate crisis*

They keep referring to that darned, two-bit break-in. But for the
loyalty of a few subordinates, the president could have said, "You're
fired." That very well could have ended it.
> *House minority leader* ROBERT MICHEL, *a Republican, in 1990 on
> Richard Nixon and Watergate*

Indecent Disclosures

This attractive lady whom I had only recently been introduced to
dropped into my lap. . . . I chose not to dump her off.
> GARY HART, *referring to an early encounter with Donna Rice,
> in 1987*

You're grown, she's grown, and you're both single. Now you may be a
faggot or something, and that seems strange.
> *Illinois congressman* GUS SAVAGE *in 1989, accused of
> sexual assault of a Peace Corps volunteer, speaking to
> reporters in Chicago*

Well, Teddy, I see you've changed your position on offshore drilling.

Senator HOWELL HEFLIN *of Alabama in 1990, speaking to Senator Edward Kennedy while inspecting a photo of Kennedy in a compromising position with a woman while floating in a boat*

Can you fault me for enjoying what you would call "the beach scene" and thinking that I could get away with it? Yep. Yep.

Senator CHARLES ROBB *of Virginia, former Democratic governor of the state, tainted by late 1980s allegations of attending parties where cocaine addicts were in abundance. In 1991, Tai Collins, a former Miss Virginia/USA, said she had had sex with Robb in a New York hotel room in 1984. Robb, who traded allegations of extramarital conduct with Virginia governor Douglas Wilder throughout 1991, insisted he had only shared a bottle of wine with her and accepted a massage.*

Well, if I had, I wouldn't tell you.

Presidential candidate BILL CLINTON *in 1992, responding to a reporter's question: "Have you ever had an extramarital affair?"*

In Europe, extramarital affairs are considered a sign of good health, a feat.

Belgian legislator JEAN-PIERRE DETREMERIE *in 1992, offering a European perspective on the controversy over Bill Clinton's denial of allegations by nightclub waitress Gennifer Flowers that she had had a 12-year affair with the governor and presidential candidate*

Fund-Raising Follies

Eggs McBentson.
> *Label given to breakfasts given by Senator Lloyd Bentsen, for which he briefly collected campaign donations of $10,000 each from lobbyists in the mid-1980s*

I thought it was a significant development for American society.
> *House speaker* JIM WRIGHT *in 1989, on why he inserted into the* Congressional Record *a plug for a motivational video by a firm that paid his wife $36,000 a year*

I told him that $3,000 was more than I can accept, and if he wants to buy books, fine.
> *House speaker* JIM WRIGHT *in 1989, on how his fee for speaking at a Texas college went to buy 504 copies of his book,* Reflections of a Public Man

---

◆

> *Men are more easily governed through their vices than through their virtues.*
>
> NAPOLEON

All of us in both political parties must resolve to bring this period of mindless cannibalism to an end.
> JIM WRIGHT *in 1989, announcing his resignation from Congress*

You know exactly who the mindless cannibal is.

> *Democratic congressman* DAVID BONIOR, *on Congressman Newt Gingrich, who originally accused Wright of wrongdoing*

The special interests that contribute to a successful campaign also expect consideration. All too often they get it.

> *Congressman* DON RIEGLE, *one of the so-called "Keating Five" senators and congressmen who were alleged in 1990 to have lobbied in the 1980s on behalf of failed savings and loan operator Charles Keating, in his 1972 published diary,* O Congress

·11·

Invective and Ridicule

JOHN MONTEGU, *Earl of*
Sandwich and member of
the House of Lords:
Egad, sir. I do not know whether you will die upon the gallows or of
the pox.

JOHN WILKES, *member of Parliament*:
That must depend, milord, upon whether I first embrace your
lordship's principles or your lordship's mistresses.

Yes, I am a Jew, and when the ancestors of the right honorable
gentleman were brutal savages in an unknown island, mine were
priests in the temple of Solomon.
> BENJAMIN DISRAELI, *British statesman, responding to a taunt by*
> *Daniel O'Connell*

A sophisticated rhetorician, inebriated with the exuberance of his own verbosity, and gifted with an egotistical imagination that can at all times command an interminable and inconsistent series of arguments to malign an opponent and to glorify himself.

> BENJAMIN DISRAELI *in 1878, on longtime parliamentary foe*
> *William Gladstone*

If Gladstone fell into the Thames, that would be a misfortune. And if anyone pulled him out, that, I suppose, would be a calamity.

> BENJAMIN DISRAELI, *asked to distinguish between a misfortune*
> *and a calamity*

I do not say that all Grits are horse thieves, but I feel quite sure that all horse thieves are Grits.

> *Canadian prime minister* JOHN A. MACDONALD, *leader of the*
> *Conservative Party. A Grit was a member of the opposition*
> *Liberal Party.*

I suppose I overdo it, but when I'm mad at a man I want to climb right up his chest.

> THEODORE ROOSEVELT

A cold-blooded, narrow-minded, obstinate, timid old psalm-singing politician.

> THEODORE ROOSEVELT, *on fellow Republican Benjamin Harrison*

When they circumcised Herbert Samuel they threw away the wrong bit.
DAVID LLOYD GEORGE, *British prime minister from 1916–1922*

Decided only to be undecided, resolved to be irresolute, adamant for drift, solid for fluidity, all-powerful to be impotent.
WINSTON CHURCHILL *in 1936, on the policies of rival Stanley Baldwin*

Yes, I am. And you're ugly. But tomorrow I'll be sober.
WINSTON CHURCHILL, *to a woman who complained that he was drunk*

Madam, if I were your husband I'd eat it.
WINSTON CHURCHILL *to a woman who admonished him, saying, "If you were my husband, I'd poison your food."*

I never give them hell. I just tell the truth, and they think it's hell.
HARRY TRUMAN

The real trouble with Stevenson is that he's no better than a regular sissy.
HARRY TRUMAN *on Adlai Stevenson*

A dumb son of a bitch.
HARRY TRUMAN *on General Douglas MacArthur*

Ike didn't know anything, and all the time he was in office he didn't learn a thing.

HARRY TRUMAN *on Dwight Eisenhower*

[Eisenhower was] no better than a coward. . . . When Castro came to power down in Cuba, Ike just sat on his ass and acted like if he didn't notice what was going on down there, why, maybe Castro would go away or something.

HARRY TRUMAN *on how President Dwight Eisenhower messed up by "losing" Cuba to the Communists. Truman, of course, had earlier suffered the accusation of having "lost" China to the Communists in 1949. Roaring from his retirement lair, Truman said that in Ike's place he would have called Castro to Washington, warned him against the Soviets, and offered U.S. assistance. "Well, he'd have thanked me, and we'd have talked awhile, and then as he got up to go, I'd have said to him, "Now, Fidel, I've told you what we'll do for you. There's one thing you can do for me. Would you get a shave and a haircut and take a bath?"*

The philosophy of the Liberal Party is very simple—say anything, think anything, or better still, do not think at all, but put us in power because it is we who can govern you best.

Journalist PIERRE TRUDEAU *in 1963. Five years later, Trudeau was elected leader of the Liberal Party, which he led to a sweeping election victory the same year.*

◆

Politics, as a practice, whatever its professions, has always been the systematic organization of hatreds.

HENRY BROOKS ADAMS

I never will ascribe to this government such wrongdoing as mere stupidity will explain.

JOHN DIEFENBAKER, *Conservative party leader in Canada's House of Commons, attacking the Liberal government in 1966*

The papers say Dalton Camp is revolting. I cannot disagree.

JOHN DIEFENBAKER, *referring to the ringleader of a group of Conservatives that succeeded in ousting him from the party leadership*

I love to make him mad. You can do it by saying, innocently, that no other member has the ability to compress such small thoughts into so many words.

JOHN DIEFENBAKER *in 1967, on Liberal cabinet minister Paul Martin*

To conceal thought he uses words. Indeed, as I listened to him from time to time I am reminded of someone in the United States Senate who described the tongue of a certain senator as being like a race horse: the less load it carries the faster it goes.

JOHN DIEFENBAKER

What is the difference between the Conservative caucus and a porcupine? Well, you see, a porcupine has all its pricks on the outside.
Deposed Conservative leader JOHN DIEFENBAKER

He has Minnesota running-water disease. I've never known anyone from Minnesota that could keep their mouth shut. It's just something in the water out there.
LYNDON JOHNSON *on his vice president, Hubert Humphrey*

He cries too much.
LYNDON JOHNSON *in 1968, describing Hubert Humphrey*

There is only one sound argument for democracy, and that is the argument that it is a crime for any man to hold himself out as better than other men, and, above all, a most heinous offense for him to prove it.

H. L. MENCKEN in 1920

Look at that face, that hateful face.
House speaker SAM RAYBURN, *watching Richard Nixon giving a speech on television*

Richard Nixon represents the dark side of the American spirit.
ROBERT KENNEDY *campaigning for the presidency in 1968*

If, in challenging, we polarize the American people, I say it is time for a positive polarization.

Vice President SPIRO AGNEW

Asking Senator Fulbright's advice on foreign policy is like asking the Boston Strangler to massage your neck.

SPIRO AGNEW

I could give no better description of this budget than to use the words of Abraham Lincoln when, in 1858, he described a budget by saying it "was as thin as the homeopathic soup that was made by boiling the shadow of a pigeon that had starved to death."

JOHN DIEFENBAKER *in 1970, attacking the government's budget*

Under the present Prime Minister parliament has been compared to a cemetery operated by its own occupants.

> JOHN DIEFENBAKER *in 1970, faulting prime minister Pierre Trudeau*
> *for his disrespect of Parliament*

If you want to see me again, don't bring signs saying "Trudeau is a pig" and don't bring signs that he hustles women, because I won't talk to you. I didn't get into politics to be insulted. And don't throw wheat at me either.

> PIERRE TRUDEAU *in 1969, on a visit to Saskatoon*

Mangez de la merde!

> PIERRE TRUDEAU *in 1970, shouting at striking federal mail-truck*
> *drivers. Translation: Let them eat shit—a variation of Marie*
> *Antoinette's reply when told the people had no bread that they should*
> *eat cake*

Fuddle-duddle.

> PIERRE TRUDEAU *insisted in 1971 that this was what he had said in*
> *parliamentary debate, when opposition members were certain he had*
> *mouthed an obscenity*

There are still people in my party who believe in consensus politics. I regard them as Quislings, as traitors. . . . I mean it.

> MARGARET THATCHER *in 1978, one year before becoming prime*
> *minister of Britain*

If the minister of finance had the courage and the conviction of a garrotted gerbil, he would resign tomorrow. He is worse than a castrated lemming today, he is a garrotted gerbil.

> *Canadian member of parliament* JOHN CROSBIE *in 1980, referring to adversary Allan MacEachen*

Being attacked by Joe Clark is like being savaged by a dead sheep.

> *Canadian member of parliament* BOB RAE *in 1981, on former prime minister Joseph Clark*

He looks like a lawnmower gone berserk.

> JOHN CROSBIE *on fellow Canadian parliamentarian Herb Gray*

He looks like the driver of the getaway car.

> *Progressive Conservative Party strategist* DALTON CAMP *on Liberal cabinet minister Jean Chretien, noted for his awkward gait and crooked smile*

Pierre, you're being obnoxious. Stop acting like a naughty schoolboy.

> MARGARET THATCHER *to Pierre Trudeau during a Group of Seven economic summit in 1981*

[**R**eagan is] perfecting the Teflon-coated Presidency . . . nothing sticks to him. He is responsible for nothing—civil rights, Central America, the Middle East, the economy, the environment. He is just the master of ceremonies at someone else's dinner.

> *Democratic representative* PATRICIA SCHROEDER *of Colorado in 1983*

If I were to try to read, much less answer, all the attacks made on me, this shop might as well be closed for any other business. I do the very best I know how—the very best I can; and I mean to keep doing so until the end. If the end brings me out all right, what is said against me won't amount to anything. If the end brings me out wrong, ten angels swearing I was right would make no difference.

ABRAHAM LINCOLN

You know, it's a pity about Ronnie—he doesn't understand economics at all.

> MARGARET THATCHER *on Ronald Reagan in 1983, following the Group of Seven economic summit at Williamsburg, where Reagan had watched* The Sound of Music *on television the night before the meetings began rather than reading his briefing books*

That appalling woman.

> *British Labour Party leader* NEIL KINNOCK *on Margaret Thatcher, prime minister and leader of the Conservatives*

Ted Heath in drag.

> DENIS HEALEY *of Britain's Labour Party, on Margaret Thatcher. Edward Heath is the man Thatcher replaced as leader of the Conservatives in a bitter 1975 battle.*

She has eyes like Caligula and the mouth of Marilyn Monroe.
French president FRANCOIS MITTERRAND, *a socialist, on Margaret Thatcher*

We shouldn't be bothered by her. She is just a middle-aged hysteric.
SHINTARO ISHIHARA, *member of the Japanese parliament, on French Prime Minister Edith Cresson's frequent attacks on the threat posed to Europe's economy by the Japanese, whom she has described as "ants"*

An amiable dunce.
Former defense secretary CLARK CLIFFORD *in 1981, on Ronald Reagan. Clifford invited similar descriptions of his own conduct a decade later when questioned about his role in running an offshoot of the corruption-ridden Bank of Credit and Commerce International.*

How boring is he? It's said that if he were going down for the third time, someone else's life would flash before his eyes.

> *A line that made the rounds of the Ontario leadership convention of the Progressive Conservative Party in the mid-1980s in description of Dennis Timbrell, a leading contender*

When one's left wing is not working, one tends to fly around in circles a great deal.

> BOB RAE, *socialist premier of Ontario*

Just quiet down, baby.

> *Canadian justice minister* JOHN CROSBIE *in 1985, in Commons debate. The barb was directed at opposition parliamentarian Sheila Copps. At the time, Crosbie was responsible for laws respecting the equality of women.*

I don't think we ought to judge one another's soul. I'm not going to judge Ronald Reagan and ask, "Why did you leave your first wife? Was that a Christian thing to do? Have you seen your grandchild?" I don't want to judge his soul or his conscience. . . . I'm not going to debate Ronald Reagan on whether he's a hypocrite.

> *New York governor* MARIO CUOMO *in 1984, asked if he believes Reagan is a "good Christian"*

I absolutely believe President Reagan when he says he does not want to establish a state religion—that would require him to attend services.

> *Senator* DANIEL PATRICK MOYNIHAN *of New York in 1984*

I was up in New England the other day, campaigning in Vermont, and I said, "It's nice to be here in Vermont when the sap is running," and one of the pickets stood up and said, "Stop talking about [Walter] Mondale like that.

GEORGE BUSH *campaigning in Indiana in 1984*

If ignorance ever goes to $40 a barrel, I want drilling rights on George Bush's head.

Texas agriculture commissioner JIM HIGHTOWER *in 1988, campaigning for Michael Dukakis*

We were being led by a team of people with good intentions and bad ideas, people with all the common sense of Huey, Dewey and Louie.

> RONALD REAGAN *in 1985, comparing the Carter administration to Donald Duck's relatives*

What you have here is an Administration that has set its hair on fire and is trying to put it out with a hammer.

> Senator ALFONSE D'AMATO *of New York on the Reagan administration's failed attempt to oust Panamanian dictator Manuel Noriega in 1988*

The Secret Service is under orders that if Bush is shot, to shoot Quayle.

> Senator JOHN KERRY *in 1988. Kerry later apologized for repeating the widespread joke about the vice president-elect.*

Bush and Bush.

> *New York governor* MARIO CUOMO *in 1988, asked to think of the weakest GOP ticket he could imagine*

People would say, "We need a man on the ticket."

> *Democratic congresswoman* PATRICIA SCHROEDER *in 1988, on why George Bush is unlikely to select a woman as his running mate*

[Vice President Bush] appears to be a Charlie McCarthy. He has no views of his own.

> *Nevada governor* PAUL LAXALT, *in 1988*

[**H**e's a] Boy Scout with a hormone imbalance.

> *Republican analyst* KEVIN PHILLIPS *on George Bush*

The unpleasant sound emitting from Bush as he traipses from one conservative gathering to another is a thin, tinny "arf"—the sound of a lapdog.

> GEORGE WILL, *syndicated columnist and confidant of Nancy and Ronald Reagan, on George Bush, whom he also called a "phony" and a "panderer"*

A pin-stripin' polo-playin' umbrella-totin' Ivy-leaguer, born with a silver spoon so far back in his mouth that you couldn't get it out with a crowbar.

> BILL BAXLEY, *lieutenant governor of Alabama, on George Bush*

He sends out a message of personal instability. Bush is not seen as a stable commodity.

> DAVID KEENE, *Bush's former political director, in 1988*

Don't vote for that fuckin' Bush!

> BRUCE SPRINGSTEEN *in 1988, to the audience at a New York concert*

The hustler from Chicago.

> GEORGE BUSH *in 1988, on Jesse Jackson. Jackson responded by saying Bush had revealed a lack of stability and "would be a national risk" as president.*

I will note this is the first time the mayor is in a courtroom. He has never appeared when a commissioner was being sentenced. He has never appeared when a borough president or someone in high political office was being sentenced.

> *Judge* RUTH MOSKOWITZ *in 1988, criticizing New York mayor Ed Koch after he advocated jail time for low-level city workers who stole thousands of dollars from the city's parking meters*

I was a little disappointed in that movie *The Last Emperor.* I thought it was going to be about Don Regan.

> *President* RONALD REAGAN *in 1988, on his ousted chief of staff at a White House Correspondents' Association dinner*

Eddie, you know why [the local paper] doesn't endorse you . . . it's because you're an asshole.

> GEORGE KEVERIAN, *speaker of the Massachusetts House of Representatives, denouncing Massachusetts Congressman Edward Markey*

Pass me the tequila, Sheila, and lie down and love me again.

> JOHN CROSBIE *in 1990, on Sheila Copps. He said her candidacy for leadership of Canada's Liberal Party reminded him of an old song.*

What do you do if you're in a room with Muammar Qaddafi, Saddam Hussein and John Sununu and you have a gun that has only two bullets? Shoot Sununu twice.

> *Former presidential candidate* MICHAEL DUKAKIS *in 1990, on White House chief of staff John Sununu, his nemesis in the 1988 campaign*

Finis! Finished! Done! Out the door, Barney!

> California Congressman ROBERT DORNAN in 1990,
> during a House debate on how to punish Congressman
> Barney Frank of Massachusetts for his relationship with a
> male prostitute

There is no man so blessed that some who stand by his deathbed won't hail the occasion with delight.

> MARCUS AURELIUS

Cabin boy.

> MARIO CUOMO's tag for Dan Quayle, a remark that neatly obscured
> Cuomo's own 1991 budget impasse in Albany

If the founding fathers had adopted this definition of revolutionary change, America would still be part of England.

> RICHARD GEPHARDT, Democratic majority House leader, faulting
> George Bush's proposed education reforms as ineffectual, in 1991

This was a better day for Kodak than it was for our kids.

> TOM ANDREWS, Democratic congressman of Maine,
> dismissing President Bush's appearance at a Lewiston,
> Maine, classroom as a meaningless photo opportunity,
> in 1991

◆

Public opinion in this country is everything.
                                        ABRAHAM LINCOLN in 1859

I won't say he flew a lot. But he won't start a cabinet meeting until
the seat backs and tray tables are locked into the upright position.
          Senator ROBERT DOLE *in 1991, on White House chief of staff*
                                                   John Sununu

Swearing is an art form. You can express yourself much more
directly, much more exactly, much more succinctly, with properly
used curse words.
          Detroit mayor COLEMAN YOUNG *in 1991, defending his frequent use*
                                                   of expletives

I can assure you my checks don't bounce. No offense, Newt.
          Senator JAY ROCKEFELLER *of West Virginia in 1991, at a party*
                   attended by Congressman Newt Gingrich, one of the many
                   congressmen revealed to have bounced checks at the House of
                                            Representatives' bank

I didn't vote for you, I didn't even think of voting for you and I
probably won't next time.
          ROBERT STRAUSS, *newly appointed U.S. ambassador to Moscow and*
                   former head of the Democratic National Committee, expressing
                   gratitude to George Bush, the man who appointed him to the

diplomatic post. Bush replied: "You're the first person to say that to me since I've been sitting behind this desk. That's why I want you for the job."

All those bad things I said about you, Dan, when I was a Democrat—like most things Democrats say—should be ignored.
> BUDDY ROEMER, *Louisiana governor and Democrat-turned-Republican, apologizing to Vice President Dan Quayle in the course of a failed bid to win the GOP nomination for governor in 1991*

Wait a minute, will you, curly?
> ERNANI BERNARDI, *Los Angeles city councilman, who is white, to black councilman Mark Ridley-Thomas, during a 1991 council debate*

Stop being Mr. Nice Guy. When you're nice, it just makes me want to throw up.
> BARBARA CARLSON, *Minneapolis radio talk-show host, to her guest and ex-husband, Governor Arne Carlson, in 1991*

If you want anything said, ask a man. If you want anything done, ask a woman.
> MARGARET THATCHER

She will have to get her ecstasy of orgasm some other way. She will have to achieve that elsewhere—maybe with a vibrator.
> ERNIE CHAMBERS, *Nebraska state senator and an opponent of the*

death penalty, on the efforts of assistant attorney general Sharon
Lindgren to obtain a death sentence for a convicted murderer in 1991

Dressing is a matter of taste, and I've met very few Republicans with good taste.

> WILLIE BROWN, *California assembly speaker and sartorially attuned*
> *Democrat, in 1991*

He's the only man I know who could look at the swimsuit issue of
Sports Illustrated and complain because the bathing suits weren't flame retardant.

> JAMES BAKER, *George Bush's secretary of state, on Michael Dukakis,*
> *in 1991*

What a slut.

> *Canadian member of parliament* WILLIAM KEMPLING *in 1991,*
> *attacking Liberal Party deputy leader Sheila Copps*

Shut up, Sambo.

> *Attributed to Canadian member of parliament* JACK SHIELDS,
> *apparently directed at the House of Commons' only black member,*
> *Howard McCurdy, in 1991. Shields denied making the remark, but*
> *apologized for unspecified comments.*

Fucking bastard.

> *Attributed to* BRIAN MULRONEY *in reference to an opposition member*

during Commons debate, in 1991. Asked later about the remark,
Mulroney said only that "I have no time to deal with trivia."

A candidate who devotes as much time talking to either himself or the heavens.

Presidential candidate TOM HARKIN *in 1991, on will-he-or-won't-he candidate Mario Cuomo*

He's large and he's slabby and he's cold.

EDMUND MORRIS, *presidential biographer, on spending time with Ronald Reagan, in 1991*

You have all the characteristics of a popular politician: a horrible voice, bad breeding, and a vulgar manner.

ARISTOPHANES, *Knights*

Who is this chickenshit?

GEORGE BUSH *in 1991, on Senator Paul Wellstone of Minnesota*

I am sick and tired every night hearing one of these carping little liberal Democrats jumping all over my you-know-what.

GEORGE BUSH *campaigning in New Hampshire in January 1992. Rolling out what he described as his "red meat" vocabulary, Bush used the trip as an occasion to lash out at "mournful pundits,"* "smart-aleck columnists," "egghead academicians," "jacklegs jumping up demanding equal time with some screwy scheme" and "tired subcommittee chairmen in Washington, D.C., who haven't had a new thought in the 50 years they've been sitting there." Among these powerful Democrats, presumably, is Bush's frequent golf companion Dan Rostenkowski, head of the House Ways and Means Committee—one of many Democrats who can attest to Bush's preference for bipartisanship during nonelection years.

He doesn't seem to stand for anything.

RONALD REAGAN *in March 1992, summing up his view of candidate George Bush. Reagan later denied making the remark, which was first reported in* The Washington Post, *but the former president then refused to be seen with the president in public, skipping a Los Angeles fund-raising event for Bush and barring the press from his house when Bush visited. A senior official in the White House told a* Newsweek *reporter "Reagan was too senile to make an appearance." One GOP official said of the apparent snub, "It will take weeks, and a lot of extra time and money, to repair that damage."*

We were taught not to back down. Whatever our positions lost in logic might be recovered with invective.

PATRICK BUCHANAN *in his autobiography, on how his outlook has been shaped by arguments with his father at the dinner table*

Post Partum

Best wishes to Burger King, Home of the Whopper. Love,
Richard Nixon.

> *Note left behind by the former president after a visit to a New Jersey*
> *fast food restaurant in 1986*

Come to think of it, things won't be that different after all.

> *Lame duck president* RONALD REAGAN *in December 1988,*
> *contemplating a retirement in which he planned to "lean back, kick*
> *up my feet and take a long nap" at home in California*

I'd like to see people, instead of spending so much time on the ethical
problem, get after the problems that really affect the people of this
country.

> RICHARD NIXON *in 1989, remarking on the spate of political scandals*
> *arising from the failed savings and loan crisis*

At least when I was governor, cocaine was expensive.
Former California governor JERRY BROWN *in 1989*

Hey, if Barney Frank can come out of the closet, I can come out of the suitcase.
Former House speaker TIP O'NEILL *in 1989, on the mild controversy over his many commercial endorsements, including one in which he pops out of a piece of luggage*

But here, among friends, I'll say, if you hear of another deal like that, let me know.
Former president JIMMY CARTER *in 1989, alluding to his refusal to join the criticism of Ronald Reagan's million-dollar speeches in Japan*

I have often thought that if there had been a good rap group around in those days, I would have chosen a career in music instead of politics.
RICHARD NIXON *in 1990, on a tape-recorded tour of the Nixon Library*

People have misconceptions about me. They thought I was going to end up in a hospital in despair. But I looked 20 years younger. I look like a Greek god.
Former mayor ED KOCH *in 1990, about life after being voted out of office*

You go to bed every night knowing that there are things you are not aware of.

> RONALD REAGAN, *reflecting on his White House years,*
> *in 1989*

I have friends who live there and they tell me it's very nice.

> RICHARD NIXON *in 1990, asked to comment on the Watergate*
> *apartment complex in Washington, D.C.*

Nancy and I are sorry to learn about your illness. Our thoughts and prayers are with you. God bless you.

> RONALD REAGAN *in 1990, in a letter to Augusta Lockridge*
> *after she was blinded in the soap opera* Santa Barbara.
> *Lockridge is a fictional character.*

There were mistakes made that could have been avoided, and many of the things that we did could have been done better.

> MIKHAIL GORBACHEV's *final address to the nation as*
> *president of the extinct Soviet Union, on Christmas*
> *Day, 1991. At this moment of the 73-year-old*
> *Communist regime's passing, Gorbachev could not bring*
> *himself to say he was actually stepping down from the*
> *presidency, and maintained that his efforts to keep the*
> *Union together and the Communist Party in power were*
> *"historically correct."*

I would have made a good Pope.

RICHARD NIXON

Index to Quoted Sources